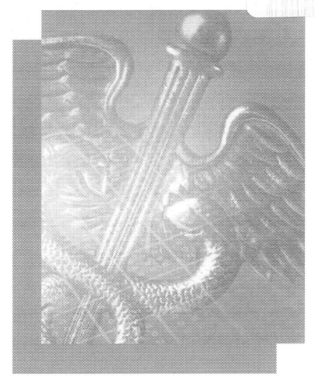

The Swift Production
Of
Powerful HealthCare Instruction

Jared Bruce Schaalje
Flathead Valley Community College

Front Cover Image, Back Cover Image, and First Page (Title Page) Image:Photo Credit:
Courtesy of Getty ImagesRights-managed and royalty-free single images78429693
(RF) Medical caduceus symbol and EKGCollection: Comstock ImagesPhotographer:
ComstockFile Size: 1022 KB - 724 x 482 pixels - RGB /Getty Images

Trafford rev. 12/09/2010

 www.trafford.com

North America & international
toll-free: 1 888 232 4444 (USA & Canada)
phone: 250 383 6864 ♦ fax: 812 355 4082

This book is dedicated to those intellectual, wise, brilliant, and amazing women who have had a profound and wonderful influence on me. Without their leadership, example and stewardship I would never have been able to write this book.

Thank you for touching my life:

Stephanie Memmott-Schaalje, Lois Schaalje, Kim Scadlock (Schaalje), Chessie Schaalje, Joyce Memmott, Elaine Colvin, Phyllis Schneider, Virginia (Ginny) Moore, Kathy Piazzi, Danita Potter, Sandra Potter, Barb Wolstoncroft, Eileen Schaalje, Debbie Schaalje, Nancy Schaalje, Alice Allred, Sharon Lynn, Judy Skinner, Joan Cahoon and Robin Olsen.

Table of Contents

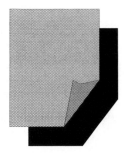

Chapter 1

High Quality, Efficiency, and the Production of Instruction

Whether you are the sole instructional designer/training developer in your hospital, clinic or other healthcare facility, or the leader/director of staff development, you can produce high quality medical education in a very short time frame. Quick production of quality learning products has numerous tangible and intangible benefits. Speed and high quality, however, seem to be two terms that are exclusive of each other. It is difficult to be quick (and inexpensive) without sacrificing quality. Likewise it is difficult to have high quality when attempting to be quick and cheap.

High quality learning products, in many instances, are extremely time consuming, costly, and may also require large amounts of planning, designing, programming, graphics, and engineering. However, high quality instructional experiences are desperately needed in the healthcare workplace. There is a strong demand to continually educate nurses, pharmacists, physical therapists, radiology technicians, insurance coders, human resource personnel, managers, executives and all others involved in caring for patients, as well as those employees who support the care providers. Meaningful learning experiences, however, are often forgone due to lack of time, money, engineering, expertise, and design. Thus, learners are often left with instructional sessions that are disjointed, unorganized, slapdash, lacking clear focus and highly inefficient.

These shoddy educational endeavors frequently find safe haven in the shelter of excuses labeled "lack of resources." In spite of providing indigent learning situations, many involved in the "low resource" instructional production process take pride in the fact that their product(s) were "efficiently" produced in a short amount of time.

Consider, for example, when the SARS virus suddenly sprang into existence and gained worldwide attention. Many hospitals, at that time, scrambled to meet regulatory training requirements by sloppily throwing a presentation together. Hundreds of doctors, nurses, receptionists, medical assistants and other key employees were herded into one large room together, to partake of a 2-hour deluge of boring facts, contained on presentation slides crammed full of text.

Low resources are NEVER an excuse for instructional indigence. Yet, frequently low-budget products (and even many high budget products) lack coherence, direction and organization. They often provide unpredictable, anxious and inefficient learning environments. A common idiom states that "something is better than nothing". However, in the world of healthcare where time carries an extremely high monetary value, nothing is usually better than wasting time on a "poorly designed something".

The methods, principles, procedures and tools presented in this book are intended to leave the instructional designer, medical staff trainer, nurse educator, clinical supervisor, medical school professor, and all others involved in healthcare learning, with no excuse! Even when financial resources are nearly non-existent (or even extinct), the practical tools and methods in this book can still be used to produce VERY HIGH QUALITY, organized and efficient instruction . . . and produce it FAST!

The benefits of producing great education in a short time are innumerable, and obviously cannot be elaborated sufficiently here in this book. Some important benefits of particular significance, however, should be noted. These include (but are not limited to) . . .

- Time savings

- Cost savings

- Reputation (both personal and hospital department)

- Peace of mind.

Time Savings

Time savings refer to saving weeks, months (and even years) in the development of good instruction. Huge amounts of time are frequently lost and wasted in academic settings such as medical schools and nursing schools, as well as in large hospitals, when attempting to design and produce certain online and classroom programs for a "pilot" to satisfy the goals of the "committee" or the "task force". Time is often lost and wasted because of low productivity during the conceptualization phase, where the "hospital committee" or "hospital task force" has no clear idea of the finished product. These groups also waste time and resources with their endless changes, revisions, updates and additions to the instruction. Finally, even more time and money is wasted when the instructional product gets caught in the "never quite finished" cycle of endless beta testing! The hospital training material, or healthcare college course, is just not finished and still imperfect.

The methods in this book present a practical instructional design template and production process, which should completely eliminate any beta testing, poor conceptualization, and endless updates. Moreover, these methods will help healthcare training departments, and academic medical institutions, to reduce their need for meaningless, ridiculous expressions such as "empower", "task-force" and "pilot study". These absurd and unintelligent business terms are often used to obscure the fact that their committee is slow, and is wasting precious organizational resources.

Many of these committees are not only incompetent at producing a tangible learning program, but likewise fail to yield a true return on investment. By using the methods in this book, however, the hospital committee will be able to actually manufacture something that is valuable to the institution, and complete it in an very short time frame.

There will be no more need for the committee to make imbecile excuses for their hospital CEO, such as "The reason we are taking so long to get you our finished product is because we are working towards developing a collaborative shared vision of core values by empowering the task force with a pilot study to explore how to best frame and shape this instruction . . . blah, blah"

Instead, the committee can say "we knew what we wanted, we built it quick, and it's yielding great results in knowledge and skills improvement." Moreover, the committee members can look their hospital CEO in the eye, and confidently tell her that "we completed this training project in half the time you gave us".

Cost Savings

Cost savings refer to saving money due to improved labor (better, more efficient on-the-job performance), and also in the drastically reduced instructional development expenditure. The practical methods in this book can be successfully used to produce amazing training with little or no budget!

One real-life example of cost savings actually happened at a large Midwestern hospital. This incident involved mandated safety and patient privacy training. This particular hospital had previously purchased a very expensive vendor-produced online training program. All doctors, nurses, allied health professionals, and support staff were required to complete this training every year, by law. The vendor's online program was poorly designed, very lengthy, and featured large amounts of irrelevant information. Moreover, it was taking physicians (the highest paid employee group) an average of about 1.5 hours to complete the course. One very sharp manager decided she would calculate the current cost of this safety/patient privacy training. She obtained a hospital-wide average hourly wage, and multiplied this by the average time to complete the course(s). Then, this number was multiplied by the total number of employees who completed the training. The total cost of this mandatory education was astoundingly high!

This manager then commissioned her instructional designer to work closely with the health system's internal subject matter experts, and come up with a solution (eLearning product) that would satisfy legal requirements, and also get to the "heart" of the most important concepts and eliminate irrelevant information. In a short time, a learning product was developed which cut the training time substantially. Hospital employees were not completing the required education in 10-15 minutes, instead of 1.5 hours! Moreover, these employees were reporting a meaningful learning experience, and their test scores revealed a solid understanding of regulatory safety procedures and patient privacy. When the same total cost was calculated, the hospital saved about $300,000 compared to the previous year. The employees were also very happy at being able to learn a lot in a short time frame.

By being solely, or partially, responsible for saving your hospital large amounts of money and time, while still meeting standards for high quality instruction, your reputation is bound to be positively affected.

Reputation (personal reputation and hospital department reputation)

While not a tangible, measurable benefit, reputation is nonetheless present (real) and exerts a powerful influence on your performance and attitude in the healthcare facility. Reputation also strongly determines the attitudes and performances of those who work close to you. When you, or your team, is responsible for developing an important training product (e.g. SARS, HIPAA, Radiation Safety, etc.) that benefits the whole organization, and is well-received, the morale in your department is bound to be more positive.

Most adults, particularly adults in a busy and stressful healthcare setting, are motivated to learn when they can master a lot of material, with a high degree of accuracy, in a very short time frame. Unfortunately, many lengthy hospital training courses purport to use principles of adult learning by involving the participants in inefficient break-out group discussions (pooled ignorance), guided exploration and discovery to find the correct answer(s), and team presentations of their "discoveries". Many of the participants are upset and bitter as they emerge from such workshops, complaining that their time was wasted and that they took hours to discover cute concepts, which could have been presented in 5 minutes. Conversely, many doctors, nurses, pharmacists, and other professional have provided highly positive feedback about learning environments where they mastered the content in a very short time frame, and didn't waste their precious working hours on meaningless "group reflection" activities. Indeed, one of the factors that can make learning exciting, and even addictive, is when a participant clearly grasps new concepts without taking huge amounts of time to do so.

Peace Of Mind

Peace of mind, the final benefit mentioned here, refers to feeling calm and organized. Feelings of calmness, as a result of utilizing the methods of this book, happen because both the production and learning process are fast, simple, and organized. With regards to peace of mind, consider the hypothetical example of a hospital supervisor or manager charged with staff training, or an academic medical educator charged with developing curriculum, who both use the procedures in this book. She will have peace of mind because her instruction for the whole year will be designed and developed fast (thus allowing her more free-time), and the results of all student learning will be objectively and quickly scored (within minutes). Moreover, her students will learn efficiently without expending unnecessary energy, and they will learn effectively with a high degree of accuracy.

Likewise, consider the hypothetical example of a health-system instructional designer and multimedia developer who use this book to design and develop instruction. She will quickly manufacture (perhaps in only a few days) a powerful course or training module. The manufacturing process is highly organized, systematic and focused, so that the educational product is built correctly the first time, and there is no need for beta testing! Not only would this be completed in an organized and systematic manner, but the actual instructional material itself would also be methodical and systematized for the learners (hospital employees).

Finally, one last point to worth noting is that the methods in this book can be used for any subject or skill in the healthcare setting. Any subject such as pharmacology, anatomy/physiology, embryology, radiology, etc., is perfectly suited for the methods in this book. Likewise, any skill such as neo-natal intensive care, administering IV drugs, using medical coding software, entering patient information into a database, MRI safety, customer service, etc., is also completely compatible with the methods in this book.

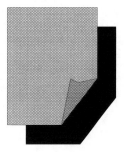

Chapter 2
Effective Instruction Defined

Before detailing the fast and efficient instructional PRODUCTION process, it is necessary to define what effective instruction is. Powerful and effective instruction has all of the following characteristics:

1. Organized

2. Digestible

3. Involves real-life scenarios where possible

4. Predictable

5. Easy to use

6. Consistent structure

7. Continuous communication of progress

8. Constant evaluation

9. Utilizes well-built selected response problems (multiple-choice questions)

10. Yields superior memorization

11. Builds critical thinking skills

These elements are all integral (super important, essential) parts of the practical instructional design templates presented in this book. These 11 characteristics of effective instruction will make learning AMAZINGLY SUCCESSFUL in any healthcare setting: clinic, hospital, medical school, nursing, or other allied health program!

The methods discussed in the subsequent chapters make it possible to speedily produce instruction (sometimes in just a few days), which contains each of these 11 characteristics. This chapter will define each of these characteristics in detail.

Organized

Organized instruction is material that is logically ordered, deliberate and designed. In other words, the placing of certain activities, lessons, information, etc., is purposeful and is all aimed at a final goal. Activities, lessons, information and other elements that detract from the main goal and do not directly influence progress, but are purely supplemental, experiential, interesting, distracting, ornamental, fluffy space-filling, and confusing should be eliminated! If they are not eliminated, then the instruction is no longer organized - it is chaotic and puzzling.

Ambiguous and esoteric goals of courses and training programs should likewise be eliminated. Organized instruction has goals that are clear, measurable, specific, and time-driven. The amount of time required for completion, or mastery, of a respective goal is specified so that a learner knows exactly how long it will take to reach a given level of knowledge, skill and expertise (competency).

Organized instruction is simple. Explanations are concise. Navigation options and buttons (if web-based), are limited and obvious. Presentations get to the point . . . and arrive there quickly! There is no unnecessary and lengthy commentary.

Digestible

Good instruction and training is presented in pieces or segments that are manageable, small and easy to digest. Similar to eating a hamburger all in one bite, many instructional programs try to "cram" as much information as possible into a given unit, segment or page. This results in confusion and frustration. Subject matter experts who have years of skilled practice, such as nurse managers, neonatal nurse practitioners, microbiologists, pathologists and surgeons, often forget what it is like to be a beginner – an unfamiliar ignoramus.

While a subject matter expert can easily digest huge amounts of information in their respective area of medical practice, it is quite a different story for an ignorant novice to be in this new learning environment with experts trying to cram as much pertinent information as possible into a given lesson. More often than not, this results in learners feeling overwhelmed, frustrated, and worst of all "behind" and unable to catch up and move on. People also tend to lose focus and "give up" or "zone out" if they feel overwhelmed and hopelessly behind. If focus is lost, then learning does not take place. If information is not focused on, it does not go past the sensory memory and enter the short-term memory, and ultimately will not be processed and filed in the long-term memory.

Similar to the hamburger analogy, if the "bite" of new knowledge is too big, it becomes frustrating and the food (knowledge) is spit out and never goes past the mouth and into the stomach (long-term memory) where it can be transformed to nutrients (skills) and fuel (useful knowledge).

A good rule to live by is Miller's (1956) law of short-term memory capacity, which is 7 plus (+) or minus (-) 2. In other words, don't give your healthcare employees or medical/nursing students more than 5 – 9 items or concepts at any one time.

However, recent research indicates that the number of new items a person is able to digest (process) at any one time may actually be closer to 2-3 pieces (Sweller et a.l, 1990; Sweller , Van Merrienboer & Paas, 1998). It may therefore be possible to overwhelm new learners with as little as 5 – 9 items. Thus, in order to make your instruction truly digestible, there should really be no more than 3, or possibly 4, items per page or per instructional instance.

Generally, the length of any one item should be about one concise sentence, equation, simplified graphic, or explanation. The substance of a given item (piece) should not be a complex, intricate, wordy enumeration; it should be broken down and presented in simple, easy-to-digest units. If your particular point, item, graphic, equation or element (item, piece) is longer than a concise sentence, then BREAK IT UP! If it takes more than one page of 3-4 concise items (bullet points) to make your point, then spread out your points over more pages. 4 pages of concise information is better than 1 jam-packed page!

Involves Real-Life Scenarios Where Possible

Powerful learning, which produces the ability to transfer new knowledge to actual on-the-job performance at a hospital, comes when relevant real-life scenarios are used. It is in using real-life scenarios that ideas, concepts, and skills become useful entities that are connected to contexts; instead of disconnected and disparate ideas. The disclaimer "where possible" is used here because there are many instructional programs in healthcare where involving real-life scenarios is neither necessary nor economically viable. Some legitimate training goals in healthcare, simply necessitate memorizing and comprehending facts. Moreover, there are instances where presentation of real-life scenarios (especially famous or familiar ones at your hospital) may be unethical and violate HIPAA privacy laws.

However, where it is possible, ethical and economically feasible, real-life scenarios should be utilized because they give the learner a chance to apply what they have learned in a relevant, useful manner. Real-life scenarios allow students and healthcare employees to see how they can change their behavior and improve their actions, when they return to the "real world" and have to face similar situations as those encountered during training.

Real-life scenarios or stories should either contain errors (obvious and subtle), or else model ideal/best practices. These scenarios involve well-developed and well-written stories, which illustrate a particular point or set of points. Scenarios or stories make it possible to include many points at once, while still maintaining interest and focus. This is because stories tend to captivate a learner's attention more than dry material facts. Large amounts of information can be encapsulated in a story or dramatization. These stories should be given only after the prerequisite skills or "dry material" are mastered, so that they have meaning to the learner.

Stories which contain errors, involve persons making one or more key mistakes (blunders). The learner is required to listen to an audio dramatization of the story, or read about it, or watch a movie about it. After the story has been watched (listened, read), the learner should then be directed to detect what errors were made, and predict the consequences of those errors. This builds higher order cognitive skills, or what is also called critical thinking or problem solving aptitudes.

An example of this type of instruction, in the neo-natal intensive care unit, could involve first completing a lesson with concise facts about inserting a catheter into an infant's umbilical cord, and then watching a movie where a doctor or nurse makes some (or many) common mistakes inserting the catheter into the umbilical region of the infant. This movie would obviously involve a mannequin or fake patient. The new NICU employee would need to detect what error(s) were made, and then predict/identify the likely consequences of those errors.

Inferring or predicting consequences involves going beyond the "present" story and deciding on the most likely "future" consequences of those errors committed. Going beyond the scenario helps students to become better critical thinkers and problem solvers. Continuing with the example of a NICU employee getting trained . . . after the new neo-natal employee has identified the errors, he/ she could then watch other short movies of possible consequences, and select the movie(s) that represent the most likely negative outcome.

Conversely, learners may also view ideal examples with no mistakes, which model best practices in real-life scenarios. In these instances, it is useful to identify the lack of mistakes, and then to predict the "positive" consequences of such actions.

Using real-life scenarios helps students to better memorize knowledge, and make it a useful part of their daily activities (transferring the knowledge to on-the-job performance). In other words, using real-life scenarios helps ensure that your instruction will effect a lasting change on the patient care provider – healthcare employees will act, think, perceive, or behave different because of completing your particular program!

Predictable

Predictable learning environments are efficient learning environments. Efficiency means accomplishing a lot, in an accurate manner, in a short amount of time. Efficiency and predictability may likely be so intertwined that it is impossible to have one without the other. When a nurse or medical student knows exactly what to expect next on a particular lesson, and there are no surprises, they are already "prepared" for the next step and can hit the ground running. "Hitting the ground running" means that they can move on to the next concept, well prepared and fully ready to absorb the new material.

Predictable environments help a learner to better get into the "focused mode", where learning and accomplishing tasks becomes enjoyable and streamlined. This state of learning, where the task is pleasurable and efficient (as opposed to frustrating and laborious), is very motivating. Dry course content actually becomes interesting and exhilarating. When healthcare employees, allied health students and others get into this focused mode, they find predictability, order, and ultimately a deep comprehension of their particular body of knowledge, whether it is microbiology, biochemistry, IV administration, or methods for restraining dangerous patients.

It is comforting for a hospital employee to know that they are accomplishing a large amount of work (or mastering a large amount of course material), in a short amount of time. ONLY in predictable environments are learners are able foresee the next step, anticipate it, prepare for it, and then accomplish it quickly and accurately.

It is therefore impossible to be efficient and accomplish very much that is worthwhile in chaotic, unorganized, unpredictable "surprise" environments, such as many of those found in universities, conference workshops, and web-based learning programs.

What is desperately needed in live hospital classrooms, medical and nursing schools, and healthcare online training, is the proper application of simple, consistent predictable structures, to a body of knowledge (subject, topic). Please see the diagram later in this chapter, for a clear visual explanation of applying simple, consistent-predictable structures to a body of knowledge. Many more people would succeed academically, and in the hospital workplace, if instructors, and others involved in the instructional design process, knew how to consistently use a simple predictable structure to organize and present their course content. In terms of instructional design, if your goal is for learners to attain a high state of focus, motivation, efficiency and peace of mind, this can ONLY be attained when a piece of instruction is predictable!

In a predictable environment, a student knows how much they have accomplished at any given point in time, and how far they have to go before they are finished. They always know where they are. This is motivating and essential, because they don't have to exhaust cognitive resources remembering useless little details.

Very frequently, learners are required to remember so many details of a pointlessly complex training activity, or remember so many purposeless particulars in their professor's course syllabus, that all or most of their cognitive resources are used up before they actually focus on the "real content", the heart of the information.

This is the known as the improper application of structure to a body of knowledge. It is improper (incorrect, less effective) because the structure is inconsistent, arbitrary, and needlessly complex. It is improper (incorrect, less effective) because the structure does NOTHING to help the students grasp large amounts of content in a short time.

The improper application of structure to a body of knowledge will increase anxiety. Anxiety is caused by not knowing what to expect, or feeling out of control. It is caused by not knowing WHY to expect the next step, and not knowing HOW to prepare for it. How can anyone feel confident and excited when a course seems pointless, chaotic, arbitrary, complex, and exhausting to keep track of tiny ridiculous details. Predictable learning environment reduce, if not completely eliminate, anxiety. Any activities in a predictable, efficient learning environment are deliberate, fit within the organizational scheme, and meaningfully contribute to acquiring large amounts of relevant information in a short amount of time.

Thus, many (if not most) cutesy activities that many trainers and professors seem to almost militantly embrace and defend, should be eliminated! Most of these cutesy and graded activities tend to confuse and overwhelm students and, moreover, misdirect them! These improper activities and course structures may likely cause healthcare employees, especially during boring mandatory safety training, to lose focus on what is most important. Thus, the training program, or university course in a healthcare curriculum, becomes a "hoop" to jump through . . . something to endure . . . a requirement. Instead, learning should be perceived as a privilege and an inspiring intellectual growth experience!

It cannot be overstated . . . the proper application of a consistent, simple structure to a body of knowledge will make learning predictable. Predictable learning environments will solve a myriad of instructional, behavioral, assessment and motivational problems.

Easy to use

How long does it take before someone can thrive and easily navigate within your learning environment, without ever becoming lost? If it takes a long time, or even more than a few short minutes, your instruction is not very usable (user friendly). At a popular retail store with thousands of locations across the United States and Canada, it was observed that some shoppers walked directly into a glass door, "bonking" their face uncomfortably against the glass. Upon being questioned as to why this happened, one shopper remarked "I thought that the right side was where people usually entered." This shopper had indeed tried to enter the doors on the right side, but at this particular store the entrance was on the LEFT, and the right side was automatically sealed shut so it could only be used as an EXIT. The automatic opening ENTRANCE doors were on the LEFT. Thus, the shopper walked directly into the non-opening EXIT doors and smacked his face on the glass. Does this seem strange that a store would be designed this way?

A very large population, in many parts of the world, drive on the right side of the road. This same throng also enters doors on the right, and walks on paths and through crowded malls on the RIGHT SIDE. Why then, would a designer who wanted to attract customers, make a difficult and uncommon route to enter a store?

Many of us involved in healthcare hospital training, and university health education, commonly do UNCOMMON things for weird reasons! This makes the heart of our course content difficult to access. Learners frequently become confused, lost, and do not know what to do next. It is important to remember those commonly used symbols, paths, habits, and other behaviors, which are shared by most human individuals . . . and use them! Use them in the design of your hospital instruction or medical/nursing school semester course.

Sometimes being too creative and unique ends up sacrificing effectiveness and learning power. It is more important for instruction to be effective and powerful, than for it to be creative and unique. This is not to say that the aesthetic, romantic, creative and brilliantly artistic do not have a place in effective healthcare instruction. Without a doubt, there is a vital place for the masterful and artistic combination of elements in instruction. However, do not make students do something uncommon, or navigate in an overly strange way, just to be different and creative. This may end up doing more harm than good. In short, make sure that it is very easy to navigate between activities within the instructional structure or "unit", and ensure that is easy to go from one particular unit to the next segment.

Consistent Structures

Closely related to predictability . . . is consistency. Consistency fosters predictability. When structure is applied to a body of knowledge, it should be applied to the whole body of knowledge, and not just to random parts that the hospital trainer, or medical school professor, likes. For example, if a matching activity is used to help memorize content in Part 1 of a pharmacist training course online, then it should also be used in approximately the same place/time in Part 2, Part 3 and so on.

The only variation that occurs is the content located within the parameters of the consistent structure. For instance, the actual questions within the matching exercise of the pharmacist online training course, will change (vary) from Part 1 to Parts 2 and 3 of the program. However, even though there are variations in the test questions, the structure of having a matching activity in each same part of the program, remains constant.

With effective instruction, the chapters, content, and presentation delivery will vary, but the structure won't. The presentation of new content will only happen in its proper "place" within the structure. The learning activity will only happen in its proper place within the structure. In this way, a learner can quickly and efficiently move through material and anticipate his or her next actions.

If the structure constantly changes, students won't know when to cognitively prepare for absorbing new information, practicing skills, memorizing, making inferences, etc. The improper and inconsistent application of structure to knowledge, happens when a different design is used on some parts of the course, but not on others. The following diagram explains this concept.

Consistent Application Of Structure Diagram

Inconsistent Application of Structure Diagram

Diagram Explanations – Consistent vs. Inconsistent Structures

The large ovals represent a particular(respective) body of knowledge. Each particular shape on the large oval represents an application of some structural element toward understanding that body of knowledge. Thus, each shape symbolizes some type of instructional activity. Each shape is in a particular "position/location" within the structure (base, top, middle, etc). The location of a particular shape is positioned with respect to the body of knowledge, and represents its relevance to the body of knowledge, Thus, on the consistent diagram, each "shape", or instructional activity, is relevant to the body of knowledge because it is located within the body of knowledge and does not go outside the boundaries. In other words, it contributes to the main goal or purpose of the course, which is ultimately to master the relevant content. On the inconsistent diagram, however, some "shapes", or instructional activities, fall outside the body of knowledge and are irrelevant to the main goal or purpose of the course (detract from mastering important course content).

The structures on the first diagram are consistently applied throughout the same body of knowledge. The structures on the second diagram are all different, and none are applied in the same place, or even consistently, throughout the body of knowledge. By the time the learner reaches the third application of structure in the first (correct) diagram, their movements through the course become much more automatic, predictable and efficient. Thus, more cognitive resources can be used to focus on the new information, rather than on the structure. Conversely, by the time a learner on the inconsistent (incorrect) diagram reaches the third application of structure, he or she has no idea what is expected in each "position", and has to spend valuable (and limited) cognitive capacities figuring out the system and activities, instead of focusing on the content. There is no chance for a learner in the second (inconsistent structure) diagram to develop automatic movements through the course course or body of knowledge. Students in the consistent diagram, however, are able to find order, patterns and a common algorithm in the instructional process. Students in the inconsistent diagram find chaos, frustration, confusion, lack of purpose and have trouble focusing!

One very likely reason for the "bell" shaped curve of student outcomes in many (if not most) courses, where the majority of students are "C" or "just average", is because a very large majority of instruction is designed using the inconsistent structure model! Thus, only a select few learners actually succeed, most just survive, and some fall away completely and drop out. Instruction that is designed using the consistent structure model, however, yields student outcomes where the MAJORITY SUCCEED and only a small minority simply survive and drop out. Having the majority succeed, however, does not always occur in healthcare training programs, as evidenced by one medical student who remarked that their college slogan was "C=MD" during medical school. . . just aim for a earning a simple "C" in your classes, and then you'll get your MD. Don't worry about trying to learn and get an "A" grade. What a tragedy! Sub-par education is often happening at our most expensive healthcare institutions – medical schools!

Content itself, like the natural world, is never consistent. This can be observed by examining the chapters in many academic textbooks. Some chapters are 30 pages long, while other chapters are 96 pages in length.

To compensate for this natural inconsistency, and still apply consistent structure, it may be necessary, for example, to apply 5 "consistent structures" for a certain chapter, while another chapter may only need 1 "consistent structure", to master the medical information.

Therefore, although nature, content and concepts are never consistent in their respective lengths, we learn best when instruction is consistent. Contextual inequality is NO EXCUSE for instructional inconsistency. Don't place an activity in its wrong location . . . this makes learning inefficient, ineffective and frustrating.

Continuous Communication of Progress

Continuous communication of progress is composed of two parts: knowing exactly where you are in a course, and knowing exactly how well you are doing at that point. It is necessary to know, at any given time, how far you've come and how much you have left before you finish. And, when clearly informed of your location in the journey, it is absolutely essential to know if you are "on-track", or missing the point(s) completely. Learners should have access to these answers IMMEDIATELY, at any time during the learning process. It is completely unfair, and poor instructional practice, for a learner to be surprised that he/she is getting an "F" at the end of the semester or training course. Likewise, it is unfair, and pathetic instructional practice, for the learner to be constantly "surprised" at how much longer they have left to go before they are finished a given unit or section, because this information is not communicated by the instructor(s).

It is motivating for learners to continually know how well they are doing and where they are. Moreover, this is a powerful means for the learner to experience continuous skill improvement. If a learner is constantly aware of where they need to improve, they can make continuous incremental improvements during the learning process, and ultimately end up like a Toyota . . . built perfectly the first time!

The structure of grading in a healthcare course should be simple. It should not be some complex scheme of points, arbitrarily assigned to hundreds of little cute and pointless assignments – that is reserved for public grade school education, as well as some ambiguous fine arts subjects, which have no clear goals or outcomes. But this is healthcare!

Complex, weird grading schemes are commonly found in many public grade school classrooms and college courses, and these schemes make it virtually impossible to provide students with any useful, immediate feedback about their current progress. This is because there are so many little pointless details to remember, account for, and earn points for. The student has to constantly remember (mentally juggle) hundreds of details and points, and the teacher has to spend large amounts of time figuring out grades in this complex-cutesy-ridiculous system. By the time the teacher is able to give any type of useful feedback, the student(s) are usually too far into the other course material, and such feedback is outdated and meaningless.

With effective instruction, there should NEVER be statements from the instructor such as . . . "the students should already have an idea of where they are, and how they are doing, so I don't need to give them constant progress reports" . . . or . . . "It's their own responsibility to keep track of their own progress. They just need to learn responsibility. I'm simply trying to empower them."

These imbecile statements assume that students have vast amounts of cognitive resources to keep track of the instructor's complex course structure, while still maintaining focus on the important course content (information). Success in this environment is difficult at best, and students anxiously spend their mental energy, and valuable time, trying to figure out the course system. In this chaos, hardly any intellectual vigor can be spared to focus on the actual course subject-matter!

Is it any wonder why the bell curve is so prevalent in public grade school (K-12) education across the United States and Canada, where instructional methods suck, and where teachers have no idea about how to design lessons that cater to human psychology, perception and cognition! Public grade school education will always continue to SUCK, as long as principles of effective instruction are neglected. Unfortunately, many students who could otherwise be successful, will continue to think that they personally "suck" and that they are a failure, because they tragically associate self-esteem with academic failure in this wretched learning environment taught by incompetent and pathetic teachers who know nothing about human cognition!

The very few "elite" will be the only ones able to succeed in this public school environment, and they will receive praise and recognition from their feckless grade school teachers. Thus the bell curve will be preserved from one generation of inept public educators, and administrators, to the next! Public grade school education in the United States and Canada will remain forever backwards. However, healthcare education in hospitals, clinics, medical schools, nursing schools and allied health programs does not, AND WILL NOT, follow the paltry, pathetic example of American and Canadian public education! We are different. We are cutting edge. We will be better than the system we grew up in.

There will be NO MORE BELL CURVE in healthcare education! A huge majority of learners will succeed in healthcare, because of powerful instruction! Nobody will ever feel that they personally "suck" when they enter into the healthcare learning arena! Self-esteem of healthcare learners will be bolstered, their confidence will be built, and ultimately patient care will be greatly improved because of this!

By providing immediate feedback about current progress, anytime within the course, and not placing this responsibility on the students, the healthcare learner's limited cognitive resources are freed up to focus on what is most important. . . the course content!

While immediate feedback about performance is important, it is likewise essential to provide information about the participant's exact "current position" in the training course.

Exact current position in a course, means that at any time a learner will know how much content, and how many activities, they have to plow through, before the course is finished. They will also know exactly how much, and what, they have accomplished thus far. This is motivating for a learner! They are less likely to lose focus/attention, and more likely to retain their desire to persevere, when they know where they are. The end is always in sight, and they can be proud of their accomplishments thus far.

When there is constant communication of progress, there will likely be no confusion in the student's mind about their grade or training program score. They will know why they received an "A" or a "B" or a "98%" or a "60%", etc. They will also know where they are going and where they just came from. This element of constant communication reduces frustration and anxiety, and brings peace of mind to the learner.

Constant Evaluation

Closely tied to the idea of constant communication of progress, is the characteristic of constant evaluation. During the 1980's, and continuing even to this day, Japanese car manufacturers applied the concepts of Total Quality Management. Among other things, Total Quality Management (TQM) applied the practice of continuous inspection (evaluation) during every step of the manufacturing process (Creech, 1995). While American motor companies were backwardly inspecting their finished product(s) at the very END of the manufacturing cycle, the Japanese were assessing each individual stage ALONG the path, and, moreover perpetually improving the practices of each phase on this path. The result for the Japanese (Honda, Toyota, Diahatsu, Isuzu, Mazda), was a nearly perfect car for their consumers. The result for the Americans (Ford, Chevrolet, Oldsmobile, General Motors, Dodge) was defective cars with transmission, engine, electrical and body problems that would cost constantly cost consumers large amounts of money in maintenance. From the 1980's until today (2010 . . .), America's car manufacturing industry has never fully recovered from it's massive loss of customers – intelligent consumers who chose high quality Japanese vehicles over clunky American automobiles.

Pride and arrogance continue today, just as in the 1980's, with American motor corporations who purport to have now invented their own "better" and "superior" brand of TQM. Thus, instead of learning from and collaborating with the Japanese, American motor companies continue to neglect powerful principles of continuous evaluation and constant quality improvement. Ironically, TQM was originally invented by a brilliant American statistician, W. Edwards Deming. Before approaching Japanese car manufacturers, he approached some American motor corporations with his revolutionary ideas of Total Quality Management, and was wholeheartedly rejected by arrogant and pompous America auto industry leaders. Thus rejected by his own people, Deming approached Japanese car manufacturers.

Here in Japan his ideas were respected, welcomed, and humbly implemented. The results were astounding and have positively affected car manufacturing, as well as many other industries, even to this present day. In our current era, when most people think of Toyota, they think of concepts such as quality and reliability. However, when many people ponder their feelings for American motor corporations, some popular acronyms humorously come to mind, such as F-O-R-D = Found On Road Dead, or F-O-R-D = Fix Or Repair Daily! Many consumers do NOT associate high quality and reliability with brands such as Ford, Chevrolet, General Motors, Oldsmobile or Dodge.

Effective instruction must likewise have continuous inspection, constant assessment and ceaseless evaluation, during every step of the learning cycle. As American/Canadian healthcare providers and American/Canadian health educators, we must NOT follow in the footsteps of our vainglorious and big-headed leaders in the U.S. automobile industry! We must NEVER reject the powerful principles of Total Quality Management (TQM) as they apply to education and learning.

Instructional inspection, or evaluation, must be systematic and not the more common "hit and miss" approach found in public schools, where only parts of the content are actually tested. Constant evaluation systematically includes all parts of the subject matter being taught. Similar to mowing a lawn, where the gardener uniformly and methodically mows over each and every area of the yard in rows to make sure that all grassy areas are accounted for and mowed over, constant evaluation also "mows" over every area of the content uniformly. If it's included in the healthcare course or hospital training program, then it's evaluated!

Continuous communication is vitally important, so that these constant evaluation measures can be relayed instantaneously to the learners. In this way, the student can make immediate course corrections (TQM), and emerge from the educational learning process (manufacturing process) as a perfect and high quality healthcare employee (perfect Toyota). The following diagrams illustrates this concept . . .

Instruction With Constant Evaluation Diagram

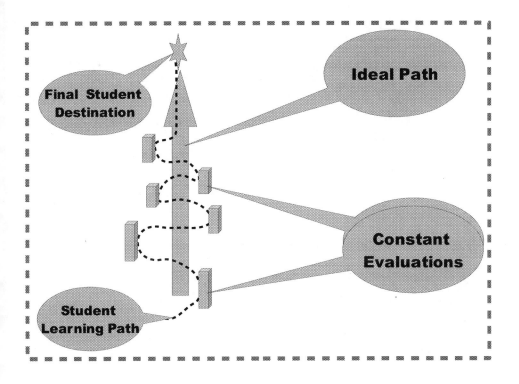

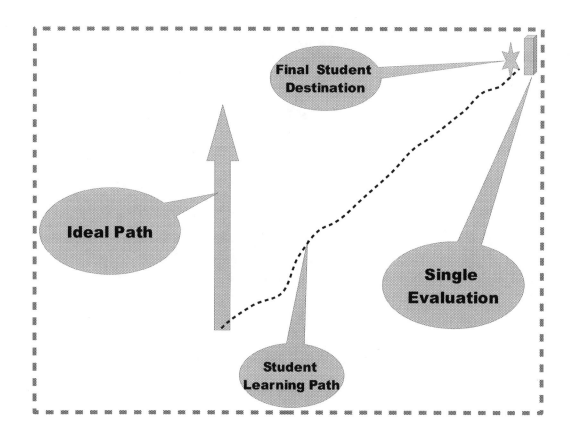

Instruction Without Constant Evaluation Diagram

Explanation of Diagrams - With / Without Constant Evaluation

As evidenced by the diagrams, constant evaluation throughout the whole instructional process causes the student to perform at, or very near, the highest standard (Toyota, Honda). Whenever performance strays, the student is regularly corrected and "brought back" to the correct path. However, without constant evaluation throughout the whole instructional process, straying from the performance standard is likely to occur, producing end-behaviors that are far from what is expected or ideal (Ford, Chevrolet).

Utilizes Well-Built Selected Response (Multiple-Choice) Problems

Selected response problems come in various types. These can include only one single-correct answer, choose-all-that-apply, true/false, matching, and context-dependent (e.g. read the following story and then answer the next 5 questions). While these types of problems are commonly used to ASSESS student learning, they are also very powerful tools for LEARNING. Indeed, multiple-choice questions are not only good for testing, but also for the actual instruction itself.

Much learning happens while a healthcare employee participates in a selected response exercise. The hospital worker is often more focused during a selected response activity, than when he/she is simply (passively) viewing material that is being presented.

Selected response exercises make it possible to give IMMEDIATE and OBJECTIVE feedback, in both classroom and web-based online learning environments.

These capabilities for providing immediate feedback make selected response problems an ideal method for efficient acquisition of skills and knowledge. This is because the immediate course correction (feedback) provides support structures and reinforcement, as learners grow in their proficiency and expertise. Effective instruction rarely, if ever, uses the more traditional (and crappy) "figure it out on your own" approach, which provides little or no scaffolding, support and feedback. This crappy, and lazy, approach is reserved for the public schools.

Selected response problems provide a measure of cognitive scaffolding/support by giving immediate feedback, and by providing the correct answer among highly likely distracters. Distracters are the plausible, but incorrect, answer options that the learner chooses from.

Many persons worry that selected response instructional activities give the student a chance to "guess" their way to the correct answer. This is a fallacy! It is very unintelligent to refer to these types of questions as "multiple-guess", because they are NOT! If there are 3 distracters (plausible but incorrect answer choices), and 1 correct answer, the student's chance of RANDOMLY guessing the correct answer on that ONE SINGLE PROBLEM is ¼, or 25%. However, if there are 10 multiple choice questions, with 3 distracters and 1 correct answer each (per question), then the learner's probability of RANDOMLY guessing the correct answer for ALL TEN PROBLEMS is ¼^10 (1 over 4 to the 10th power), or 1/1,048,576.

This means that the student has a 0.0000954% chance of just "guessing" the correct answer for all 10 of these questions. The student has a 1 in one-million forty-eight thousand five-hundred and seventy-six % chance of merely guessing all answers correctly! It is simply

NOT going to happen . . . a student is NEVER going to guess the correct answer to all 10 questions at random.

Selected response problems can be used for memorization of facts, as well as to expand and improve critical thinking abilities. Not only can a selected response problem help a student to remember and recall important information, but it can also be constructed to help the healthcare scholar to reason, analyze, synthesize and solve complex problems. Reasoning, analyzing, and creating (synthesizing, innovating) are critical thinking skills. Selected response instructional activities are a powerful means to memorize and learn to think critically, about information in medical settings. Later in this book, clear instructions will be provided for constructing selected response activities that help healthcare students memorize, analyze and predict.

Yields Superior Memorization

Effective Instruction must result in superior memorization of relevant facts, skills, procedures, knowledge, concepts, etc. It is very difficult, if not impossible, to think critically about healthcare situations, if foundational facts are not infused permanently into memory. Critical thinking is the purposeful and deliberate recombination of memorized facts, to creatively reach certain novel and original goals.

To help illustrate the need for memorized facts before thinking critically, consider the example of a medical lab pathologist. It is highly improbable that a pathologist could make a difficult diagnosis (critical thinking) of cancer from a tissue sample, if she was unable to combine her foundation of memorized facts such as parts of cells, chemical reactions, typical cell shapes, cell growth/division cycles, etc. Moreover, she would also need to have memorized strategies for reasoning, analyzing, and diagnosing other similar types of cancers. The pathologist had to first have a foundation of memorized facts, in order to reason and think critically about this unique tissue sample that is possibly cancerous.

The very act of critical thinking (higher order cognitive reasoning) itself, involves combining memorized facts, methods, objects, and subjects to reach a desired outcome. Reasoning at higher levels of intelligence is currently a primary focus at many schools of nursing. This is wonderful, and is evidence of the cutting edge of healthcare education! In order to think and reason at these higher levels in all healthcare subjects, there must always be a strong foundation of memorized knowledge that is readily accessible, available and retrievable at any time.

The word "superior" is used because effective instruction produces learners that have memorized the content to a high degree of mastery. A high degree of mastery is when an individual can recall and remember large amounts of information, long after the course or training program is finished. Moreover, the healthcare student has memorized the information in a "superior" fashion when he/she can recall the fact(s) and information ANYTIME it is needed to solve important problems.

This means that the nurse practitioner will be able to recall vital information when he is super exhausted at 3:40 a.m., and wants to go home and sleep. This likewise means that 12 years after the medical student has completed her course in pharmacology, she will still be able to provide her patients with advice about anti-psychotic drugs.

Simply reading a textbook, as the sole method of information acquisition, will NOT produce superior memorization. Being told a HIPAA (healthcare patient privacy) concept only once, in a crowded lecture hall with 340 other hospital employees, will NOT result in competent, superior memorization. Superior memorization of information comes when an individual is exposed to content in a manner that is organized, small enough to digest, predictably structured, and uses systematic selected response items as both a means to constantly evaluate mastery levels, and also as a learning activity(s).

Builds Critical Thinking

It has been established that there is a need for memorization, as a prerequisite to critical thinking. Critical thinking is the final hallmark of powerful instruction. Instruction must provide the means and the activities for new interpretation, prediction, creative application, analysis, extrapolation, thoughtful reasoning, exploration of new possibilities, and intriguing questioning of new content. It should not stop at memorization alone. Critical thinking activities should always happen at the same place, within a predictable framework or "structure of activities", each time the structure is applied in the lesson.

Critical thinking activities should always come after pertinent, relevant and necessary knowledge has been memorized, and never be interspersed arbitrarily at random places in the instructional structure. Within the consistent instructional structure, memorization activities are a cue for learners to anticipate and prepare for the higher level reasoning (critical thinking), which will shortly follow.

Critical thinking activities may involve real or contrived stories, which provide a context (setting, background) for the particular piece of new information. As stated under this chapter's heading titled "Involves Real Life Problems Where Possible", error detection or ideal best practice scenarios, are excellent critical thinking activities that allow learners to see the application (or misapplication) of concepts, and identify them. These scenarios not only give learners the opportunity to detect errors, but also provide a thought provoking opportunity to predict the consequences of the actions, and/or infer the meaning from the certain behavior(s) in the story.

These critical thinking stories can be effectively portrayed in mediums such as live role plays, written stories, audio dramatizations (similar to old-time-radio dramas), movies, newspaper articles, or picture slide shows with narration. Each medium has its advantages and disadvantages. When selecting a medium to present a critical thinking activity, choose the one that best stimulates thought-provoking emotions/responses, but also clearly conveys the story. Critical thinking is important because it helps healthcare employees to contemplate cause-and-effect, to question common assumptions and look for flaws in their logic, to think about new "what if's", and ultimately to make new discoveries and inventions. Critical thinking helps learner to avoid over-simplifying and romanticizing, and to realize the vast complexities that underlie causes.

Conclusion

Powerful instruction can be produced quickly, without sacrificing quality, as long as some crucial elements and characteristics are included in the design. When these elements and characteristics are ALL included, healthcare students and hospital employees can achieve a high level of skill and knowledge mastery. They can enjoy a satisfying and exciting learning experience. Moreover, they will maintain focus without having to waste limited cognitive resources on irrelevant, inconsequential, and unimportant details, which are a part of so many other incompetent learning environments.

Effective instruction is organized,digestible, involves real-life scenarios, is predictable and user-friendly, has a consistent structure, continuously communicates progress and assessment scores, utilizes multiple-choice activities, yields superior memorization, and ultimately builds critical thinking skills in the healthcare workplace. When these elements are included, your hospital employees will leave your training program having a firm grasp of the content. They will apply what they have learned, and ultimately improve patient care!

Reference

Miller, G.A. (1956). The magical number seven, plus or minus two: Some limits on our capacity for processing information. *Psychological Review, 63*: 81-87.

Sweller, J., Chandler, P., Tierney, P., & Cooper, M. (1990). Cognitive load as a factor in the structuring of technical material. *Journal of Experimental Psychology, General, 119*: 176-192.

Sweller, J., Van Merrienboer, J.J.G., & Paas, F. (1990). Cognitive architectures and instructional design. *Educational Psychology Review, 10*(3): 251-296.

Creech, B. (1995). *The five pillars of TQM: How to make total quality management work for you.* New York: Penguin Books, USA Inc.

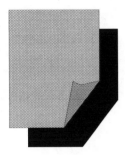

Chapter 3
The Information Course Template

Information courses present content (subject matter, course material) in an exciting, systematic, and organized fashion. Each information course is a short "unit of instruction" with the following:

1. Introduction

2. Information/interaction

3. Memorization

4. Verification

These 4 phases, or stages, constitute an information course. A course can also be referred to as a unit, a module, or a section within (as part of) a complete PROGRAM. Thus, a complete "program" may have one, or many, information courses (units, modules, sections), depending on the scope of the program. The purpose of an information course is to methodically memorize the subject matter. These courses can be either a prerequisite to a critical thinking course, or simply an end in itself (the final destination).

As mentioned previously, critical thinking is the hallmark of powerful instruction. Many times, however, healthcare learning needs are fulfilled simply with an "information" course. There are instances where a critical thinking course may not be cost-effective, or even necessary, to fulfill certain healthcare training objectives.

An information course may also be a preparatory online course in a medical school, to gear up students for more advanced hands-on clinical training. An information module may be used to prepare emergency medical technicians with a foundation of necessary memorized knowledge, so that they can participate in critical thinking simulations when they come to the classroom. Again, the most effective instructional programs will have both an information course and a critical thinking course. The critical thinking course template will be presented later in this book.

As mentioned earlier, the structure of the information course consists of 4 parts. These are: an exciting introduction, the information/interaction phase, the memorization segment, and the verification stage. Each of these 4 parts will be explained in detail. There will also be a clear description of how these are combined together to form a complete and powerful unit of instruction.

This "information course" method of designing instruction employs these 9 elements of effective instruction, mentioned in the previous chapter:

1. organized

2. digestible

3. predictable

4. easy to use

5. consistent structure

6. continuous communication of progress

7. constant evaluation

8. utilization of selected response learning activities

9. superior memorization

When a critical thinking course is combined with this information course, then the remaining two elements of effective instruction (real-life scenarios and building critical thinking skills) are also employed. Throughout the explanation of the activities in the information course, each of these elements of effective instruction will be referenced, and it will be shown how these characteristics are put into practice (made operational and practical).

Exciting Introduction

The introduction, or better called the "exciting" introduction, is the FIRST part of the information course. The introduction is intended to increase predictability, by showing the learner what is coming up in the unit. In some ways, this exciting introduction is similar to a movie preview . . . you get a taste of what the movie is about, and become stirred up with positive feelings toward the subject matter. The introduction, in an information course, will briefly introduce the healthcare learner to the upcoming topics, and help motivate him/her by using appropriate music and animations. Short movie clips, brief humorous role plays (in a classroom), and other media may be used in the exciting introduction phase of the information course.

In a computer-based (online learning) environment, which is a very common component of many medical schools, nursing schools and large hospitals, exciting introductions may often include such elements as:

- Letters and words animating and morphing (changing shape) into different objects and pictures

- Deliberate repetition of key phrases and words throughout an animated sequence. Such as "see no evil, hear no evil, speak no evil" when introducing a lesson about HIPAA patient privacy

- Relevant pictures or graphics of the upcoming content, presented in a montage with cool music

- Words and phrases that fade in and fade out, timed to music

In a hospital training auditorium, or a nursing school classroom with live (face-to-face) instructors and trainers, an exciting introduction may include elements such as:

- Live, quick demonstrations, such as a fun chemical reaction

- Brief stories that captivate the learners and illustrate the upcoming content

- Short DVD (movie) clips

- Role plays or live dramatizations that are humorous

Important guidelines to remember when making exciting introductions, include the following:

- Keep it short and extremely relevant

- Make sure topic headings of the information presentation pages are included in the introduction, where possible. Topic headings will be shown later in this chapter

- Use music, movies, and animation, where possible and appropriate, so that the upcoming subject matter is exciting, predictable and memorable for the learners

- Be sure to have an "exciting introduction" for EVERY information course (unit, module) in the medical training program. This makes for consistency, organization, predictability and efficient acquisition of knowledge

Teachers may often use exciting introductions for only certain units, and fail to use them for other lessons. This results in a disjointed instructional structure applied sporadically to the body of knowledge, and inefficient and unpredictable learning for healthcare students.

The elements of effective instruction that are operationalized (realized, made concrete, become tangible and practical) in the "exciting introduction" phase of the information course include:

- Predictability

- Communication of progress. An exciting introduction informs learners of how far they have come and of what they are about to attain in their journey to expertise

- Consistent structure. The introduction is ALWAYS the FIRST part of the structure of instructional activities, which are applied to the body of knowledge

Information/Interaction

The information/interaction phase of the "information course" is SECOND phase of an information course. This is where the actual content is communicated (presented) to the learners. As evidenced by the information/interaction diagram shown later in this section, there are 3 pages of content, followed immediately by a learning interaction AFTER the 3rd

page. A learning interaction can be a true/false question, a choose-all-that-apply multiple choice question, or any other type of selected response activity, which is immediately and objectively scored. Regardless of the healthcare setting for the information course (online or classroom), the "pages" are formatted in the same manner. This will be explained in more detail shortly.

At this point, it is most important to gain a macro or "big picture" view of the information/interaction phase of the "information course". Here is the big picture:

- There are three pages of text information, followed by a learning interaction on the 4th page

- A "set" consists of 3-pages of text, and 1 learning interaction

- In an information course, there are NO MORE THAN 4 SETS! If more information needs to be presented, then CREATE A BRAND NEW INFORMATION COURSE

- On each individual page of text, there is a brief title followed by NO MORE THAN 3 BULLET POINTS per page

- Each "bullet point" should be no more than 1-2 sentences

- Each page of text should aim to be, more or less, like a billboard . . . a learner can IMMEDIATELY and QUICKLY scan and read through all the material. Just like a billboard is designed so that the freeway driver can discern the message in 2-4 seconds, each text page should likewise be quickly and immediately discernible

- The multiple choice question on the 4th page (learning interaction) is derived from the content on the FIRST of each 3-page set. Later in this chapter we will discuss how the other two pages, in each 3-page set, are assessed systematically

- Since the content that is farthest away from the learner's conscious memory is the text on the FIRST of each 3-page set, this is what is included in the learning interaction

The following diagram illustrates a "set" in the information/interaction phase of the information course . . .

Diagram Of A "Set"

Heading (Title)	Heading (Title)	Heading (Title)
- Bullet Point 1	- Bullet Point 1	- Bullet Point 1
- Bullet Point 2	- Bullet Point 2	- Bullet Point 2
- Bullet Point 3	- Bullet Point 3	- Bullet Point 3
Page 1	**Page 2**	**Page 3**

Learning Interaction, Derived from content on Page 1

Diagram Of COMPLETE Information/Interaction Section, ALL 4 SETS:

Heading (Title)   **Heading (Title)**   **Heading (Title)**

- Bullet Point 1
- Bullet Point 2
- Bullet Point 3

Page 1   **Page 2**   **Page 3**

Learning Interaction, Derived from content on Page 1

Heading (Title)   **Heading (Title)**   **Heading (Title)**

- Bullet Point 1
- Bullet Point 2
- Bullet Point 3

Page 1   **Page 2**   **Page 3**

Learning Interaction, Derived from content on Page 1

Heading (Title)   **Heading (Title)**   **Heading (Title)**

- Bullet Point 1
- Bullet Point 2
- Bullet Point 3

Page 1   **Page 2**   **Page 3**

Learning Interaction, Derived from content on Page 1

Heading (Title)   **Heading (Title)**   **Heading (Title)**

- Bullet Point 1
- Bullet Point 2
- Bullet Point 3

Page 1   **Page 2**   **Page 3**

Learning Interaction, Derived from content on Page 1

Here is an example of how a healthcare content page could appear in an "information" course, in the information/interaction section:

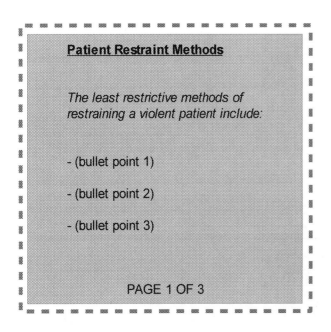

In this example of subject matter in the information/interaction section, the use of text was highlighted. However, each page of content may just as easily be communicated using audio, video, pictures, or animated lectures. All of these may be used in place of text. If audio, video or animation is used, a slightly larger amount of information can be conveyed per page, without overwhelming the healthcare learner. However, the multimedia used in place of the text should still not be overly lengthy. This means that audio explanations should not be any longer than about three to five minutes per page, and movies or animations should likewise not exceed five minutes per page.

The interactions after every third page of information should, as stated earlier, be one of four main types of multiple choice questions: true/false, single-correct answer, choose-all-that-apply, or fill-in-the-blank.

The content (subject matter) used to derive and develop each of these respective interactions must be taken from the FIRST of each of the 3-page sets. By doing this, the interactions SYSTEMATICALLY assess a specific, given area of the knowledge presented. The content from the remaining 2nd and 3rd pages of content, in each three-page set, is used to build the interactions in the MEMORIZATION and VERIFICATION phases of the information course. The memorization and verification phases will be discussed later in this chapter.

When building any of the learning interactions (multiple-choice questions), be sure they are simple "recall" questions that require the learner to simply REMEMBER what was contained on the first of each 3-page set. This is an "information" course, and the purpose of this course is for the learner to rapidly and efficiently MEMORIZE and retain important healthcare facts, figures and knowledge. Questions that require extrapolation, inference, or predicting future consequences, are inappropriate at this stage. The point of the information course is to MEMORIZE. Critical thinking comes in a latter course, when there is an adequate foundation of memorized facts to draw upon and reason with.

Effective critical thinking requires that relevant material first be permanently infused into the healthcare employee's memory, and this is accomplished through memorization activities that demand recall. These recall/remember questions (interactions) are very easy to construct, since they can be taken directly (often word-for-word) from the information contained on the first page of each 3-page set..

Elements of effective instruction that are operationalized (realized, made concrete, become tangible and practical) in the information/interaction section include:

- Predictability

- Communication of progress (the base of each page shows how much is left in the overall course, what page the learner is currently on, and how much is left in the information/interaction section)

- Consistent structure (there are ALWAYS 3 pages of information, followed by a multiple-choice learning interaction)

- Utilized properly constructed selected-response items

- Constant evaluation (the interactions constantly evaluate and assess the healthcare learner's grasp of the knowledge presented on page 1 of each 3-page set)

- Digestible (there are no more than 3 bullet points per page, so as to not exceed short-term memory capacity)

- Organized

Memorization

The MEMORIZATION phase is the third portion of the information course. The memorization phase is simply a matching activity. Each matching pair is taken from the 2nd page, of each 3-page set in the information/interaction section.

The memorization section is a fun phase, and gives the healthcare learner a chance to make mental associations through "matching" ideas, concepts, and facts contained in the 2nd page of each of the 3-page sets in the information/interaction section. This systematically evaluates the content, and ensuring that every piece of content is reinforced and reminded to the learner. The healthcare employee is thus able to re-build the second page of each three-page set, through these matching questions. An example of a matching activity, to train medical lab technicians, could appear as follows:

Match each of the following pictures of bacteria (bacterial infection) with the corresponding antibiotic that is usually chosen

(Picture A)_____	(Antibiotic B)
(Picture B)_____	(Antibiotic D)
(Picture C)_____	(Antibiotic C)
(Picture D)_____	(Antibiotic A)

Elements of effective instruction that are operationalized (realized, made concrete, become tangible and practical) in the memorization section include:

- Communication or progress (the base of each page shows how much is left on the overall course, with descriptors such as: pg. 11/24. The base of each page also shows how much is left in the memorization section itself)

- Consistent structure (the memorization section ALWAYS comes after the information/interaction portion)

- Utilizes properly constructed selected-response items (matching items are a form of multiple-choice, or selected-response, items that are immediately and objectively scored)

- Easy to use (matching questions are very easy for the learner to figure out how to use. The questions may not be easy to solve, but it is simple to know what is expected of the student)

- Constant and systematic evaluation (this section evaluates the learner's grasp of the subject matter contained on page 2, of each 3-page set, in the information/interaction section)

Verification

The verification phase is the LAST section in the "information" course, the fourth phase. This phase consists simply of single-correct, or choose-all-that-apply, multiple choice questions. The subject matter that is used to construct each of these verification questions comes from the 3rd page, of each three-page set, in the information/interaction section. Thus, after completion of the verification questions, learners will have systematically been evaluated on EVERY page of content in the information/interaction section. The healthcare learners will have systematically re-built each page of content presented in the information/interaction phase, by the time they complete this verification section. Thus, all the content has been reinforced to the healthcare learners, and they are well-prepared with a powerful foundation of facts that can be readily recalled in the hospital workplace!

A single verification learning activity (multiple-choice question) consists of a brief question, followed by 3-4 options with at least 1 (or more) correct answer(s). If possible, it is best to randomize the order that the verification questions appear to the learners, and also to randomize the order of the answer choices. It is assumed that the healthcare learner will go through the verification section more than once, until he/she attains a score of 100% in this section. Thus, if it is possible to randomize, then the healthcare learner will have a more optimal learning experience by focusing on the content, and not the order (placement) of answers and questions.

Typically, the question for each multiple-choice learning activity should be as short (brief) as possible . . . only 1-2 sentences. The questions should never use phrases such as "all of the above are correct except . . . ", or "none of these are correct except . . . " and other such confusing linguistics. Also, be sure to make each answer option as similar as possible to the correct answer(s), and try to make each distracter (plausible, but incorrect answer option) the same length as the correct answer(s). Avoid distracters such as "all of the above" or "A, C but not D" or "all but C" and other such poorly worded and confusing options. Instead, have plausible distracters that are very similar to the actual answer, with the exception of a few minor words/details. In this way, the learner is required to attenuate to minute details in the the correct answer, and will better memorize important information.

The verification section is an excellent place to provide quick diagnostic feedback to the healthcare learner, and to help him/her meaningfully distinguish the correct answer. This final verification section of the information course, is an important place for the learner to memorize the last of the 3-page sets in the information/interaction section, and to FINISH STRONG so that he/she can confidently move on to the next stage of expertise in their particular area of healthcare: pharmacy, lab tech, radiography, ultrasonography, human resource information systems, leadership, nursing, or physical therapy.

Elements of effective instruction that are operationalized (realized, made concrete, become tangible and practical) in the verification section include:

- Communication of progress (the base of each page shows how much is left in the overall course, and also how much is left in the verification section)

- Consistent structure (the verification section ALWAYS comes after the memorization portion)

- Utilizes properly constructed selected-response items

- Constant and systematic evaluation (this section tests and assesses the learner's grasp of the subject matter on page 3, of each three-page set, in the information/interaction section)

- Easy to use (verification questions are very easy to figure out, and are not a complex goofy game with quirky rules and details that distract and detract from the main content. Verification questions are simple items that have only one correct answer, or more than one correct answer)

Information Course - Healthcare Classrooms and Online Environments

The information course will work powerfully in the medical school lecture hall, anatomy lab, nursing school classroom, hospital auditorium, or enterprise web-based training system. For a computer-based setting such as a laptop in a medical library, or a cell phone/ hand-held device carried on the hospital floor, learning interactions can be immediately scored and feedback can be instantly provided within seconds. There are many amazing and powerful programs available to build these learning interactions, and also to build blank "templates" for quick production of an information course.

Many of these programs are free or open-source, some are cheap, and a number are quite expensive (more than the price of a regular computer). It is important to keep in mind, however, that amazing training can be built using free and open source programs that do not cost anything. Many of these programs come with built-in learning interactions such as drag-and-drop, hot spot, fill-in-the-blank, etc. These ready-made interactions are excellent, provide immediate feedback, and are easily customizable to your needs without having to write any actual computer code. You don't need to be a computer science major or a Java programmer to build amazing eLearning in healthcare!

Each web or interaction page in the computer-based (hand-held device) training must have a small indicator at the base of the page to display overall progress in the course, and to give a description of the current page. In the technology-mediated environment, key elements of effective instruction, such as continuous communication of progress and constant systematic evaluation with corrective feedback, are easily made possible.

A very simplified example of the graphic interface in the information course is shown as follows:

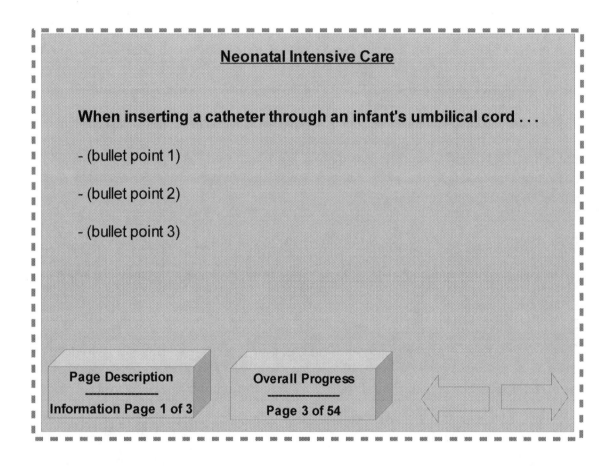

In this example, the user is shown a description of the page they are on, and what their overall progress is at this point. On the far right side, the learner can click the forward arrow to move on, and the back arrow to review previous material. This interface incorporates elements of effective instruction.

There are very few buttons, so the course is easy to use. With the information course and the critical thinking course, these two buttons (forward and back) are the ONLY ones that are

EVER needed. This makes for sound usability (user-friendliness). In this example, the user is not overloaded with information, and there is continuous communication of progress. These are elements of effective instruction!

In a hospital auditorium or medical, nursing, and allied health classroom setting, it is also possible (and VERY APPROPRIATE) to constantly communicate progress to students, and give quick (albeit not quite instantaneous) feedback on learning interactions. The method to accomplish this is quite simple. . .

First, provide all medical students with a complete paper-based packet for each respective "information course" that will be presented during the lecture series or hospital training program. It is essential that each allied healthcare student have this packet, and USE IT as part of their classroom experience. This packet makes it possible for them to follow along, and increases the predictability of the learning environment.

Each packet contains an introduction page that briefly describes how you will introduce the unit. Following the introduction page, are the information/interaction pages. After these sections are the memorization and verification pages respectively. At the base of each individual page, the student's current overall progress is shown.

When presenting in a live classroom lecture, be sure to follow each information page exactly. Do not let your presentation deviate from what is in the packet. Even though there are only four key points per page, your lecture (speaking) can expand greatly on each key point in more detail. Hospital employees and university medical students are paying to hear you speak, NOT to read the pages. Furthermore, it is impossible to pay attention to two things at once. Thus, if a student is listening to you, he/she cannot read a lengthy handout. And the reverse is also true . . . if a student is reading a lengthy handout, he/she is not attenuating to your dynamic medical lecture! Thus, keep the text on each handout very brief so that the nursing students will listen (attenuate) to your awesome lecture!

Every third page of the packet contains an interaction such as a true/false, fill-in-the-blank, or single-correct multiple-choice question. Include a separate answer sheet with the packet, where the students will "fill in the bubbles" to record their answers. The answer sheet will contain a maximum of 12 questions (4 questions for the information/interaction phase, four questions for the memorization phase, and 4 more questions for the verification phase of the respective information course). When your class reaches the FOURTH page in the information/interaction phase (the page AFTER the 3rd page of each 3-page set), where there is a learning interaction (multiple-choice question), have them take a moment to read the question in their packet, and then go and record their response on the answer sheet.

When the memorization and verification phases are reached, again have them read the questions in their packet. Then, direct them to go and record their responses on their "bubble" answer sheet.

To score each student's responses almost immediately (without the use of an expensive scanning machine, or any technology), the best method to use is the hole-punched answer key. . .

Using an bubble answer sheet identical to that of your students, punch a hole over each "bubble" that is the correct answer for each question (questions 1-12), using a hole-puncher. Then, simply lay the hole-punched answer key over top of each student's answer sheet, and it immediately becomes apparent which answers are correctly chosen (shaded/bubbled in), and which ones were missed, by the respective student.

Put a mark through the incorrect answers by drawing through the correct holes on your answer key, marking directly onto the student's answer sheet.

This method takes about 3 second's per student, to give them overall feedback for all 12 questions in the whole information course! Not quite immediate, but still very fast!

One final note. For matching activities in the memorization section, have students match the letter of each correct "association" to the corresponding number on their bubble answer sheet. For "choose all that apply" questions, have each option on the bubble answer sheet represent a list of choices, possibly similar to this example:

- A = choices 1, 2, 3, 4

- B = choices 2, 4, 5

- C = choices 1, 3, 5

- D = choices 1, 2, 3, 4, 5

An example of the graphic layout, of a page in the packet for a classroom information course, is shown in the following diagram . . .

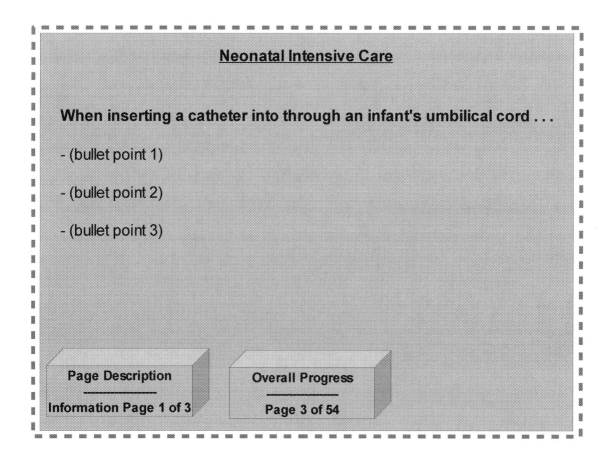

The example shown here is nearly identical to that of the computer based / hand-held device interface. This is because the elements of effective instruction for an information course are the same, regardless of the medium. The only difference between this example and the technology-mediated one, is that there is no need for navigation buttons, since the learners will be manually turning papers.

By using these methods for your medical/nursing school classroom, your future doctors and nurses will find predictability, organization, and increased ability to pay attention and follow along.

It is also very motivating to get timely and quick feedback, even if it is not quite immediate but rather at the end of each lecture or unit.

Whether your healthcare "information" course is web-based or taught in a hospital auditorium, when it finished being built it should be structured exactly like the following diagram . . .

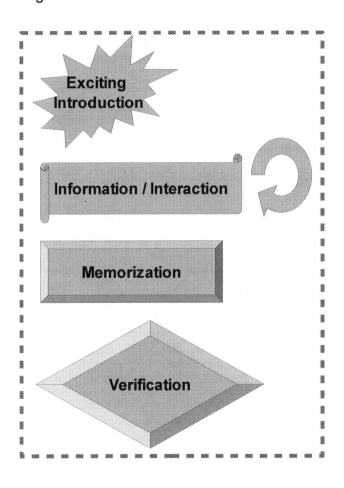

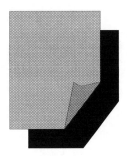

Chapter 4
The Critical Thinking Course Template

Critical thinking, in many respects, involves the ability to take previous facts,

knowledge, data, etc., and use it to infer relationships (cause and effect), predict

consequences in novel real-life situations, and analyze the improper application of knowledge

in varying scenarios. By going through exercises that involve inferring cause-effect

relationships, predicting likely consequences, and identifying the proper/improper application

of knowledge, healthcare learners will be competent, and well prepared to use their training to

improve patient care!

The Critical thinking course involves two main parts. The first part is the STORY or

presentation of the scenario. The second part is a set of 3 selected response activities, which

are immediately scored. These two parts will be explained in detail.

The story, or scenario, portion of the critical thinking course is subdivided into three

"pages" or parts. The first page is a brief introduction to the story. On this FIRST page, the

healthcare employee is told what they will see. They are told what to watch for, and also what

to think about while watching (reading, listening to) the story. The following diagram illustrates

this . . .

Scenario 1:
The Nurse Restrains a Violent Patient

- In this movie, you will see a restraint
that is incorrectly applied by the nurse

- Watch what the nurse
does and says to the patient

- Think about what you would
do differently if you were here

The second "page" of this story portion is the ACTUAL STORY or scenario, presented as a movie (motion picture), audio dramatization, slide show with narration, or simple text story. There are many ways to portray the story that are exciting and effective. At times, it may only be feasible to have a well-written short story in novel/drama format, at other times, especially in the medical school or allied health classroom, it is appropriate to have a live dramatization with students and/or professional actors. Pictures with voice narrations and music can be very effective and inexpensive to produce, and movies with internal hospital employees as the actors have often been produced inexpensively with very positive results. An audio dramatization may be a very powerful way to depict a story, as this is inexpensive, and it can also be a way to stir up emotion in the learners, especially if the healthcare issue is controversial or complex.

The scenarios or stories should involve real-life complex situations and not be contrived, over-simplified, romanticized depictions. Instead, the stories should reflect the actual complexity that is a part of everyday healthcare.

Idealized training that is formatted in a "1950's happy-go-lucky" type of portrayal, is unrealistic and stupid, and results in poor transfer of learning to the real difficult and dynamic world. The ideal is never encountered, and training course that is based on this fantasy results in acquiring useless skills and having unrealistic expectations.

The scenarios (stories) can be examples of likely errors made in difficult healthcare situations, or else they can model expert performance from seasoned professionals. Both are valuable. They should not be too lengthy, and also should not have so many details that the main point is obscured.

The third, and last, page in the story/scenario portion is the "discussion" or "reflection" page. This page includes a general description of what was just portrayed, what should (or should not) have been done, and what some general consequences could be. This page can be presented with audio/video discussion by experts reflecting on the scenario, or with regular text. Consider the following diagram . . .

REFLECTION:

The Nurse Restrains a Violent Patient

- The nurse should have done . . .

- The patient will probably . . .

- The possible legal consequences are . . .

The Second Part of the Critical Thinking Course

As stated at the beginning of this chapter, the second part of the critical thinking course is the selected response phase. The selected response portion is divided into three pieces. These sections are:

1. error detection

2. prediction

3. correction

The selected response activities are presented in this specific, exact order. The type of multiple choice question that is used EXCLUSIVELY in the critical thinking course is the choose-all-that-apply genre. NO OTHER format is of multiple-choice question (selected-response activity) is used in the critical thinking course.

Error detection activities (multiple-choice questions) require the healthcare learner to identify all specific errors committed in the story. Or, conversely, if the scenario modeled expert performance, then these activities require the learner to identify what was performed correctly in the story.

Prediction activities (multiple-choice questions) ask the medical student to prognosticate or foretell a highly probable consequence of the actions in the story. These consequences are educated guesses, based on clinical data.

Correction activities (multiple-choice questions) challenge the hospital employee to select those decisions and actions that SHOULD HAVE been made in the story, and which would have resulted in avoiding the unpleasant consequences. The learner chooses the ideal

response, as if he/she could go back in time and re-enact the story. This is a very powerful

reflection and critical thinking activity!

The following diagrams show brief examples of each of the three types of questions . . .

Error Detection

What did the lab technician do incorrectly, when he analyzed the tissue sample?

(choose all that apply)

☐ (answer option 1)
☐ (answer option 2)
☐ (answer option 3)
☐ (answer option 4)
☐ (answer option 5)
☐ (answer option 6)

<u>Prediction</u>

What likely consequences do you predict will happen, as a result of this doctor's actions?

(choose all that apply)

☐ (answer option 1)
☐ (answer option 2)
☐ (answer option 3)
☐ (answer option 4)
☐ (answer option 5)
☐ (answer option 6)

Correction

If you were the pharmacist in this story, how would you have acted ideally?

(choose all that apply)

- ☐ (answer option 1)
- ☐ (answer option 2)
- ☐ (answer option 3)
- ☐ (answer option 4)
- ☐ (answer option 5)
- ☐ (answer option 6)

As with the information course, a "set" consists of a story (with its introduction and reflection pages) followed by the 3 critical thinking questions. A complete critical thinking course consists of a MAXIMUM of 4 SETS. In the critical thinking course, there should be no more than 4 story/selected response sets. If there are any more than this, the healthcare student is likely to be overwhelmed. If, therefore, you have more critical thinking material to teach, then CREATE ANOTHER SEPARATE CRITICAL THINKING COURSE.

Diagram of a Critical Thinking Course "Set"

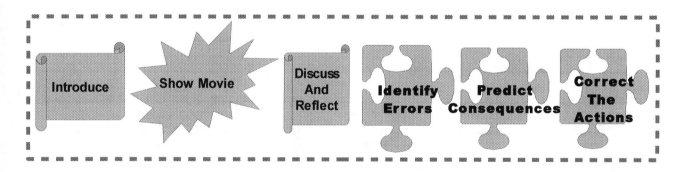

Diagram of a Complete Critical Thinking Course

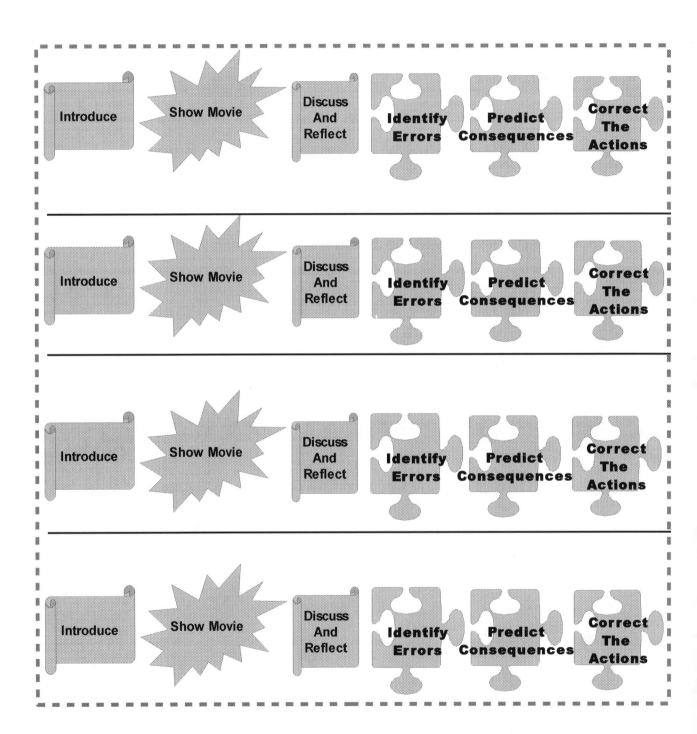

When this critical thinking course is part of a "program" in conjunction with a prerequisite information course, learners will not only have memorized the initial subject matter, but will also have had the opportunity to reason, analyze, and apply their knowledge in the healthcare workplace. These two courses, when combined together, comprises ALL the elements of effective instruction, which were named in chapter 2. The critical course is organized, uses real-life scenarios, builds higher order cognitive skills, and systematically and continuously evaluates the learner (TQM).

Critical Thinking Course - Healthcare Classrooms and Online

The critical thinking course, just like the information course, is equally effective in either a healthcare classroom such as a hospital training auditorium or nursing school classroom, or in a virtual medical learning system (online).

In the live classroom, instead of separate web-pages or computer screens for the sections of the critical thinking course, the students are given a complete paper-based packet with the complete critical thinking course. This is the exact same methodology that was used to adapt the information course for the classroom environment, as described at the end of the previous chapter. The "printed paper packet" contains the story/scenario parts (introduction, story, reflection/discussion) as well as the selected response activities printed out on separate pages (identify errors, predict consequences, correct the actions). Again, it is essential that each student have this packet, and use it as part of their classroom experience.

This packet makes it possible for them to follow along, and increases predictability in the classroom environment.

Even though the story is shown in text, on the respective page in the packet, the instructor may still show a video dramatization, have the medical students act out the story, show a slide show, or listen to an audio dramatization of it, in the live classroom setting. At the base of each printed page, the student's current overall progress is shown.

After the story portion of the critical thinking course is presented in the a live healthcare classroom, use a "bubble sheet" for students to record their answers, exactly the same way as specified with the information course. Likewise, use the punched-hole answer key method, as described in the information course section, to provide immediate feedback to your live classroom students, regarding their performance on the critical thinking questions. For the "choose all that apply" format in the bubble sheet, have each individual option (a, b, c, d) represent a series or list of choices (e.g. A = 1, 2, 3; B = 1, 4; etc.,).

The elements of effective instruction for a critical thinking course are the same, regardless of the medium (lap-top, hand-held cell phone, classroom). The only difference in the graphic interface is that there is no need for navigation buttons in the live classroom print-outs of the pages, since the learners will be turning the pages instead of clicking a mouse.

By using the methods discussed in this chapter, to design your "critical thinking" classroom or online medical, nursing or allied health course, your learners will find predictability, organization, and an increased ability to pay attention and follow along. It is very motivating to get timely and quick feedback! It is very motivating to build healthcare critical thinking skills in a TQM-Toyota type of learning environment!

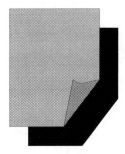

Chapter 5

Lightning-Fast Production of the Information Course

The information course can be produced efficiently, in a very short amount of time (days, in many cases). It can also be produced at a low-cost, very inexpensively. The process described in this chapter can be applied by a sole developer of online or classroom learning materials for the hospital or medical school, or a team of professionals involved in the mass manufacture of educational media. The outcome is the same, regardless of the budget or the number of individuals involved in the process . . . high quality instruction produced in a very short amount of time!

This chapter is written from the perspective of one who is overseeing the instructional development process at a large hospital, medical school or allied health program. However, these methods can easily be adapted to your unique situation, whether that is a radiology department supervisor, dean of a medical school, nursing program director, emergency medical technician instructor, or anatomy/physiology professor.

There are 4 steps involved in this "information" course production process. By following these steps exactly and precisely, you will be able to produce your high quality instruction quickly, and with little or no errors. There will be virtually NO NEED for time-wasting beta testing. The instruction will have been continuously evaluated every step of the way, and done right the first time! The steps of the production process for an "information" course are:

- idea solidification

- consultations with the subject matter expert

- subject-matter expert filling out the template (with continued guidance of the instructional designer EVERY STEP OF THE WAY, in a "Toyota-TQM" methodology from start to finish)

- converting the "subject matter expert's template" into your FINAL completed course, to be used in either a hospital's intranet online system, or in a live medical classroom lecture

Each of these steps will be explained in detail. The following SIMPLE diagram, which is a VERY EASY-TO-USE project tracking chart, will be described in this chapter:

	Step 1				Step 2				Step 3				Step 4			
%	25	50	75	100	25	50	75	100	25	50	75	100	25	50	75	100

Step 1 . . . Idea Solidification

Step 2 . . . Expert Consultation(s)

Step 3 . . . Expert Template Completion (Finish Filling Out Template)

Step 4 . . . Conversion of Expert Template Into Final Course

	Step 1				Step 2				Step 3				Step 4			
%	25	50	75	100	25	50	75	100	25	50	75	100	25	50	75	100
Course 1	█	█	█	█	█	█	█	█								
Course 2	█	█	█	█	█	█	█	█	█	█	█					
Course 3	█	█	█	█	█	█	█	█	█	█	█	█				
Course 4	█	█	█	█	█	█	█	█	█	█	█	█	█	█	█	

The Production Process For The Information Course

Each Step in the process is tracked in quarters. Thus, a medical course developer can monitor the progress of a given, respective course and see immediately if it is 25%, 50%, or 100% complete, at a certain stage of development. This progress is plotted and tracked using the simple and easy-use-chart on the previous page, by shading in the square(s) under each respective step, for the course that is currently being worked on. Therefore, if Step 1 on Course 3 had two squares shaded in, then this step is 50% completed. If all four squares are shaded in, then the step is 100% completed for Course 3. A respective course is complete, and ready to be used in the medical classroom, when Step 4 is 100% complete.

Idea Solidification

The first step in developing an information course is to solidify the idea. When an idea is solid, it is no longer a constantly changing and dynamic fluid, an ever-moving mass. It is a solid body with CLEAR BOUNDARIES of what belongs and what doesn't. A solidified idea for a healthcare instructional module means that crucial decisions are made about what to include that meets the given training goals. This is especially important when considering training doctors at a hospital. It is not necessary to include "ancillary fluff" in a training module for highly paid doctors and surgeons, when the goals for training can be met by simply memorizing a very minimal amount of subject matter. Moreover, the doctors and surgeons will be much happier when their valuable time is not wasted on dinkey frivolity!

A solidified course is a specific, focused course. This means knowing exactly which topic headings are to be used, and where they are to be placed (logical order) within the information/interaction section. Even if the course is a general, survey, or introductory type of medical training, there is still a definite idea of what topics need to be mastered, in order to have a sufficient understanding of the novice subject matter.

In order to help a medical subject matter expert have a solidified idea, introduce him/her to the overall "information course" model, the big picture. Show him/her a sample course built using the information course template, and encourage him/her to think of how many "information courses" may be needed to cover the complete body of knowledge, which they want to teach to their hospital department. Help the subject matter expert to consider what topic headings to include, and what sentences (bullet points) to write under each topic heading. The following general guidelines constitute the quarters in Step 1:

- 25% . . . A twenty-five percent solidified idea is one where the subject matter expert has a vague idea of the course title, and what the title entails

- 50% . . . A fifty percent solidified idea is one in which the course is broken down somewhat more specifically. This means that there is a more focused idea of just how many topic headings to include in the information/interaction section, and what these topic headings will be

- 75% . . . A seventy-five percent solidified idea is where the subject-matter expert has an idea of how much explanation is needed under each topic heading in the information/interaction section, to sufficiently understand each topic. This means that the amount of written text explanation, the types of media (pictures, audio, animation), and how much of each media, is decided upon

- 100% . . . A one-hundred percent solidified idea is a STABLE understanding of exactly what topics are essential to understanding the main title of the course, and what topics are supplemental fluff or not very important. This is where there is a clear idea of the BOUNDARIES of the course content. At this point, it is appropriate to move on to step 2 in the production process.

Before moving on to the next step, however, the following tool should be used to SPEED UP the process of idea solidification . . .

<u>INFORMATION COURSE - Subject Matter Expert Form</u>
(Please complete each question in the space provided)

1. What is the exact title of your course?

2. List all topics that can be included under the above title:

3. For each topic, how much explanation and teaching will be required, in order for your healthcare learners to gain a sufficient understanding? List each topic, and then write "not very much", "some", or "a lot" beside each topic, to indicate the amount of instruction needed to sufficiently understand each medical concept.

4. List each healthcare topic, and beside each topic describe the number of information text pages in the "information/interaction" section that you estimate will be needed to cover a given medical concept (topic), and what types of media (if any) will be needed to assist the learner to have a more powerful learning experience.

5. What topics can be discarded, and do not need to be included in the course? Can time/money be saved by eliminating certain activities and information, while still meeting training goals for the hospital employees?

This form should not be simply handed off to the subject matter expert, for him/her to fill out on their own, especially if this is the first time a course has built in that hospital department. Instead, you and the subject matter expert should fill this out together, at least for the first time, to ensure quality inspection every step of the way. This will ensure that that instructional products are manufactured correctly the first time. There will be no need to go back and revise, and waste more time best testing, just to see if the idea was clearly developed.

Expert Consultation(s)

While the idea solidification step requires a certain amount of discussion with the subject matter expert about the "information" course template, it is likely that the template of the information course HAS NOT been introduced in great detail during the idea solidification step. Indeed, it would have been premature to introduce and overwhelm the subject matter expert with the detailed information about the template, during the idea solidification step.

The information/interaction section of the "information" course template may have been briefly discussed during the idea solidification phase, since one of the questions on the form mentioned earlier, asks the expert to estimate the number of "information/interaction" pages needed to introduce a given topic.

During this specific phase, however, the rest of the information course template is explained, and greater detail about the information/interaction section is provided as well. Begin by showing the diagrams of a "set", and a "complete information/interaction section" as well as a "complete course", as discussed in chapter 3. This will give the subject matter expert a big picture of how all the elements fit together. In particular, discuss how the interactions in the "information/interaction" phase are all taken from the FIRST page of each 3-page set, how the memorization section contains matching activities derived from the SECOND page of each 3-page set in the information/interaction portion, and finally how the verification phase contains questions taken from the content on the THIRD page of each 3-page set in the information/interaction section.

After providing this complete view of the information course, discuss options for a powerful and exciting introduction. Recommendations for the introduction will depend on available software, medium (classroom or online), and other available resources. Be creative and original while suggesting ideas. It will take a certain amount of flexibility to come up with a good introduction, especially when resources are limited. However, it can always be done! There is always a way to have an inspiring introduction, despite the format of the course or the available nursing school budget. Be sure to tell the subject matter expert that all, or most, of the topic headings in the "information/interaction" phase of the course should be included in the introduction. The introduction is an essential component of powerful, effective instruction!

When consulting about the information/interaction phase, be sure to make clear that efficient reading and acquisition of knowledge happens when healthcare learners are NOT overloaded with information at any single instance. This is why there are only 3 key points (bullet points) per page, under each topic heading. Explain the 4 different types of interactions (multiple-choice questions) to the subject matter expert , and describe how they are used to reinforce and memorize healthcare facts/information.

While a discussion of how to effectively construct multiple-choice problems is beyond the scope of this book, it is highly recommended that you have a good book on test-item construction. This book should be a well-used reference. Some basic rules for building quality test questions should be explained to the subject matter expert, since they will the one(s) primarily involved in building the learning interactions. Construct a few ideal examples of high quality test questions, using the subject matter expert's healthcare content. This will help him/her to have a clear idea of what constitutes good learning interactions.

The memorization section is, perhaps, the easiest to build. Show the subject matter expert how to select an idea or concept from a given "page 2 of 3" in the information/interaction section, and then how to match that idea with it's correct association or definition. Explain that this section requires no construction of plausible distracters (incorrect but likely answer options), because there is only the matching of key ideas to their correct association(s). Explain that, for the healthcare learner, this is a very important part of understanding the respective topic, because the learner is making mental connections of ideas. This is a very fun activity for the learner, and an efficient means for drilling and memorizing.

The "single-correct answer" type of multiple choice questions, which comprise the verification section, are relatively simple to build. If the course is the maximum size, then there should only be 4 verification questions total. Explain to the subject matter expert that these questions are all taken from the THIRD page of each 3-page set, in the information/interaction section. Likewise, explain that ideally, each question should have 3 distracters, and one correct answer . . . making 4 choices in total (3 incorrect + 1 incorrect). Inform the subject matter to avoid "all of the above" and "none of the above" types of distracters, as these are poor distracters. Each distracter should be equally plausible (likely). The correct answer should be randomly placed among the other choices. Thus, there should never be a predictable pattern of correct answer placement. Help the subject matter understand how this verification section helps learners SYSTEMATICALLY memorize content from each of the 3rd pages, in 3-page set, and also how it helps the medical students to discriminate, comprehend and understand the course content.

The following guidelines constitute the quarters in Step 2 (expert consultation) of the lightning fast production process:

- 25% . . . Template "big picture" introduced

- 50% . . . Exciting introduction discussed. Generally decided about what to include in the introduction

- 75% . . . Exciting introduction mostly decided upon, information/interaction clearly understood and largely delineated, memorization section beginning to be discussed and decided upon

- 100% . . . Memorization section delineated and largely decided upon, verification section discussed at length and mostly decided upon, examples have been constructed to guide the subject matter in filling out the template with complete accuracy, and all parts of the blank template are clearly understood by the subject matter expert

Expert Template Completion (Finish Filling Out Template)

For the first iteration (production cycle), and preferably for all other production cycles with this same medical expert/hospital department, this stage should be done TOGETHER with you and the subject matter expert(s). The template can be either a computer form (web, online) or paper form. It can be immediately converted into your final course. To make it more user friendly, and faster to fill out for the subject-matter expert, their template is necessarily arranged different than your final course template.

The subject matter expert's template has a "blank" introduction page, where he/she clearly describes (writes) how the introduction will look, and what specific words and pictures to include. There are likewise blank information/interaction pages where topic headings and the 3 bullet points on each respective 3-page set are filled in, as well as blank interaction pages. In addition to the empty information/interaction sections, there are also fill-in-the-blank memorization and verification pages, which guide the subject matter expert to populate these spaces with his/her respective healthcare content.

The subject matter expert template, after the introduction page, has one page of information (page 1 of 3), followed immediately by one interaction page. After this, there is another information page (page 2 of 3), followed immediately by a blank memorization (matching) page. When this is concluded there is a third page blank information page (page 3 of 3), followed by a fill-in-the-blank verification page. This is how the subject matter expert's template differs from your actual course template. While your course template will consist of an introduction---information/interaction---memorization---verification, the subject matter expert's blank template will consist of this structure, for their ease of use:

1. Blank "introduction" template page

2. Blank "information (1 of 3)" template page

3. Blank "interaction (derived from pg. 1 of 3)" template page

4. Blank "information (2 of 3)" template page

5. Blank "memorization (matching derived from pg. 2 of 3)" template page

6. Blank "information (3 of 3)" template page

7. Blank "verification (single-correct multiple choice derived from pg. 3 of 3)" template page

etc., the process repeats 4 times for a complete information course . . .

Consider the following diagram (on the next page) of the subject matter expert's template, and its explanation afterward . . .

Information Page 1

(place your heading/title here)

- (place bullet point #1 here)

- (place bullet point #2 here)

- (place bullet point #3 here)

Information Page 2

(place your heading/title here)

- (place bullet point #1 here)

- (place bullet point #2 here)

- (place bullet point #3 here)

Interaction 1

(place true/false question here)

(True)
(False)

Memorization 1

(Place MATCHING question here)

(Idea/definition #1)
(Matching phrase #1); etc.,

Information Page 3

(place your heading/title here)

- (place bullet point #1 here)

- (place bullet point #2 here)

- (place bullet point #3 here)

Verification 1

(Place VERIFICATION question here)

A) (option A here)
B) (option B here)
C) (option C here)
D) (option D here)

Although the actual information course itself is not arranged this way for the healthcare students, this order (see diagram on previous page) is MUCH easier for the subject matter expert to fill out. This is because the respective subject matter expert(s) can remember and refer to the previous page(s) of information, to build the learning interaction(s) and other learning activities (memorization and verification) immediately following. This is very user friendly and efficient for the subject matter expert!

A Final Note On Continuous Quality Inspection

Even if it takes 3-5 hours to initially fill out the template together with the subject matter expert, it is much better than simply handing it off and asking him/her to fill it out on their own. By filling it out together, there will be continuous quality inspection by BOTH you (the designer) and the subject matter expert, and the finished template that is filled out correctly the first time! This means that this template is COMPLETELY READY to be built (converted) into a final course, with no need for revisions! The healthcare course is a perfect Toyota!

If the subject matter expert fills out the template on his/her own, your medical program may experience delays as the subject matter expert experiences questions (roadblocks) and frustrations, and there is a much higher chance of having errors and a need for significant revisions with the end-product healthcare course . . . you are more likely to build a Ford or a Chevrolet program for your hospital employees!

Filling out the template together greatly speeds up the production process, as well as increases accuracy.

It is a great way to implement continuous quality improvement into the instructional development process.

The following guidelines constitute the quarters in step 3 (expert template completion), assuming the course is a maximum sized information course with 4 information/interaction sets, and the corresponding amounts of memorization and verification:

- 25% . . . The diagram shown in this section, which is just ONE iteration, is filled out once. A complete information course would have this diagram (template) filled out 4 times

- 50% . . . The diagram (subject matter expert template) shown in this section, is filled out twice

- 75% . . . The diagram shown in this section is filled out THREE times

- 100% . . . The diagram shown in this section is filled out completely ALL FOUR times, and it has been FILLED OUT TOGETHER with you and the subject matter expert each time, in a manner that uses continuous quality inspection

Conversion of Expert Template Into Final Course

This step is perhaps the easiest, and the one with most tangible results. It is in this step that the course is finalized and completed. This phase consists of a fair amount of "copying and pasting" content from the subject matter expert's template into to your final course (final information course shell or template). Your final course shell or template should already have the fantastic look and feel (professional graphic design), which is demanded by your audience of healthcare learners. For a computer-based (web, hand-held/cell phone) course, the navigation and interface should already be built in a blank shell, so that the subject matter expert's content can simply be "poured" into the housing.

Your final (complete, ready-to-go) course shell or template is already in order, so this is why this step is largely comprised of copying and pasting. Your template (if eLearning) should be built in some type of an authoring program, which can be either a commercial software package, or an open-source courseware. As mentioned earlier in this book, it is entirely possible to build amazing eLearning for healthcare settings, with free and open-source software programs. Be sure to investigate these before spending large amounts of money on expensive commercial programs.

If your program is for a live hospital training setting, or a university lecture environment for a medical school or allied health program, then your final course shell can be in a word processing program or a presentation program. The content from the subject matter expert's template can be very quickly "poured" into these programs, and then the final information course can be printed out for your live medical audience.

The following guidelines constitute the quarters in Step 4 (conversion of expert template into final course), assuming the course is the maximum size:

- 25% . . . 1 subject matter expert template iteration (set) has been poured into the final course shell

- 50% . . . 2 subject matter expert template iterations (sets) have been poured into the final course shells

- 75% . . . 3 subject matter expert template iterations (sets) have been poured into the final course shells

- 100% . . . 4 subject matter expert template iterations (sets) have been poured into the final course shells

After this point, your course is built and ready to be implemented at your hospital, medical school, nursing program or allied health school!

This section outlined the lightning fast production process for the information course. If the steps presented here are followed exactly, an information course can be completed in a super short amount of time, even within days, without any need for time-wasting beta testing! This is because, as has been said many times in this chapter . . . it was done right the first time! The healthcare instructional product(s) was continuously inspected and evaluated during every step of the manufacturing process.

The next step to having a complete and effective program of instruction, which will help ensure competent doctors, nurses, pharmacists, ultrasound technicians, and others, is to add a critical thinking course to the already existing information course. The next chapter outlines the lightning fast production of the critical thinking course. This has a very similar production methodology to the one outlined here.

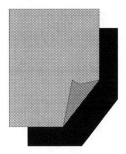

Chapter 6

Lightning-Fast Production of the Critical Thinking Course

The production process for the critical thinking course is similar to that of the information course. However, there are 5 steps instead of 4, in the development cycle of the critical thinking course. These manufacturing stages are:

- Idea solidification

- Consultation with the subject matter expert . . . discussing the critical thinking course template, making decisions about appropriate scenarios, and exploring medium(s) for portraying the stories

- Filling out the template together (designer and subject matter expert)

- Developing the scenarios (text, audio dramatization, motion picture, slide show)

- Converting the subject matter expert's template into the final course, and incorporating the finished scenarios into the completed course

Although the production cycle for a critical thinking course may take somewhat longer, because of producing the scenario portrayals (e.g. movie, audio dramatization,slide show), if the methods outlined in this chapter are followed exactly and precisely, you can still produce a critical thinking course in lightning fast time! It is still possible to produce a high quality critical thinking course within a few short days!

The diagram on the following page illustrates the critical thinking course production process. This diagram is a SIMPLE, EASY TO USE project tracking chart, similar to the one shown in the previous chapter:

%	Step 1				Step 2				Step 3				Step 4				Step 5			
	25	50	75	100	25	50	75	100	25	50	75	100	25	50	75	100	25	50	75	100

Step 1 . . . Idea Solidification

Step 2 . . . Expert Consultation(s)

Step 3 . . . Expert Template Completion (Finish Filling Out Template)

Step 4 . . . Develop Scenarios

Step 5 . . . Conversion of Expert Template Into Final Course

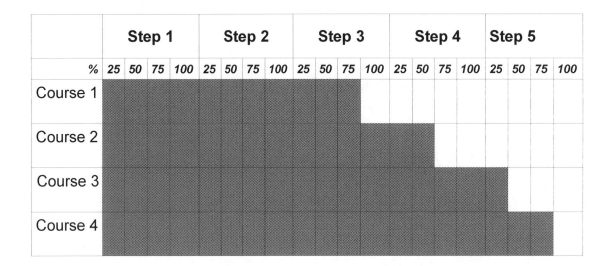

Idea Solidification

Solidifying an idea, for a critical thinking course, is nearly identical to the procedure used with an information course. When an idea for the critical thinking course becomes solid, it is no longer arrhythmic and spasmodic. It is a stable body of knowledge, with clear demarcation lines. The subject matter expert and course designer(s) know precisely what belongs, and what doesn't. Coagulated learning content (topics, subject matter) has already had crucial decisions made about what to include that meets given purposes, and what must be left out that either detracts from, or does not meaningfully contribute to, accomplishing the training goal(s).

As stated in the previous chapter, a solidified course is a specific course. Specific, for a critical thinking course, means that only relevant and focused stories/scenarios are chosen to be used in the final product(s). These scenarios are strategically and logically ordered within the course, in a prerequisite and/or hierarchical fashion.

In order to help the subject matter expert have a solidified idea of the type of course he/she wants to develop, introduce the critical thinking course model (template). After this, show him/her a sample critical thinking course, and encourage the subject matter expert to consider how many "critical thinking courses" might be needed to cover the complete body of knowledge needed for their respective hospital department, or medical school division. Assist the subject matter expert in considering the types of stories/scenarios to include, and also in pondering the content for the "choose all that apply" questions after each story.

The following guidelines constitute the completed quarters in Step 1, Idea Solidification, for the production process of a maximum sized critical thinking course:

- 25% . . . A twenty-five percent solidified idea is when the subject matter expert has a general, vague idea of the stories, and what general content to include in the choose-all-that-apply questions

- 50% . . . A fifty-percent idea is evidenced when the course is "broken down" much more specifically. This means that there is a clearer idea of just how many stories to include under each topic, and a more specific idea of what question content will help learners to think critically about the scenarios. There is also a good sense about what content to use when predicting consequences, and what content to use when identifying errors and correcting the situation(s)

- 75% . . . A seventy-five percent solidified idea is where the subject matter expert has an understanding of how much explanation is needed before each scenario, and how much discussion is needed after each story/scenario presentation, in order to help the learner prepare and reflect.

- 100% . . . A one-hundred percent solidified idea is a stable understanding of exactly what stories/scenarios are essential to meeting hospital/academic healthcare competencies , exactly what question content to include with each story(s), and how to introduce and summarize each story. There are clear bounds regarding course content. At this point, it is appropriate to move on to Step 2 in the production process.

In order to speed up the production process of idea solidification, for the subject matter expert, the form shown on the following page should be used . . .

CRITICAL THINKING COURSE - Subject Matter Expert Form
(Please complete each question in the space provided)

1. What is the OVERALL GOAL of your critical thinking course?

2. List all topics (topic headings) that are included under this goal.

3. For each topic heading, how many stories/scenarios will be required, in order to have a sufficient understanding? List each topic and then write a "0.5", "1" or "2" etc. beside each topic to indicate the estimated amount of instructional hours needed for students to think critically about each topic.

4. List each story, and beside each story describe how you will introduce each scenario, how you will summarize it, and what content you will include in the 3 types of "choose-all-that-apply" questions. These questions are "error detection" "predict the consequence" and "correct the situation" learning interactions.

5. What type of media would you like to use to portray each story (slide show with text or audio, radio show or audio dramatization, movie, or simple text story)?

This form should NOT simply be handed off to the subject matter expert, for him/her to fill it out on their own. You and the subject-matter expert should fill this out TOGETHER, even if it takes 3 hours to solidify ideas. This will save time, energy and money in the long run. This is a way to ensure continuous quality inspection during every phase of the instructional manufacturing process, for the critical thinking course. This ensures that the form is filled out correctly the first time. There will be no need to go back and revise it, or waste time doing unnecessary beta testing . . . with a "pilot" group . . . who wants to "explore" . . the feasibility . . . of the concept . . .of the idea . . . to "empower" . . . BLAH, BLAH, BLAH! None of those bagatelle, debilitating business/public education terms will be necessary in this healthcare setting. Tasks, such as idea solidification, will be performed correctly, quickly, clearly and with real purpose.

Expert Consultation(s)

The template for the critical thinking course, will probably not have been introduced in great detail, during the idea solidification phase. Thus, during this second (2nd) phase of course production: subject matter expert consultation, or expert consultation(s), the critical thinking course template is explained in exhaustive detail.

During this consultation phase, begin by showing the diagrams in chapter 4 (The Critical Thinking Course Template) of a "set" and a complete course with all "4 sets together", so that the subject matter expert can see the "big picture" of how all elements fit in concert. After explaining this large perspective, discuss specifics about how to "introduce" the overall course in an exciting manner, how to introduce each individual movie, how to summarize the respective movie(s), and what mediums are the most effective and economical for portraying the scenarios. Discuss how to provide a powerful learning experience for the healthcare employees who will participate in this training.

After deciding on the story specifics, discuss the "choose-all-that-apply" questions, and demonstrate each of the three types of questions, in exhaustive detail. Show the subject matter expert how to construct good "error detection" questions, as well as how to build fantastic "predict the consequences" and "correct the situation" questions. Work closely with the subject matter expert in a continuous quality inspection manner, to build each question carefully one-by-one. Work together to build ALL the questions that go with each respective story/scenario, throughout the whole COMPLETE critical thinking course.

The following guidelines constitute the quarters in the Expert Consultation phase, Step 2, of the critical thinking course production process:

- 25% . . . Template "big picture" diagram introduced. Elements for the "overall introduction" are chosen

- 50% . . . Template introduced in greater detail, and stories/scenarios, along with their appropriate mediums (video, audio, text, animation, slide show) have been discussed and generally decided upon

- 75% . . . Template fully understood in exhaustive detail, medium to portray story firmly decided upon, examples of the types of "choose all that apply" questions are generally understood, and somewhat decided upon

- 100% . . . Subject matter expert, with assistance of course designer, built each of the three types of multiple-choice (choose all that apply) types of critical thinking questions, for at least one of the stories/scenarios. Content for other questions is selected

Expert Template Completion (Finish Filling Out Template)

This stage should, of course, be done TOGETHER with you and the subject matter expert in a continuous quality evaluation manner. The template can be either a paper-based form, or a fill-in-the-blank online form that is accessed via hand-held electronic device or laptop with high-speed Internet access. The template is formatted so that it is super user-friendly for the subject matter expert to fill out, and also can be IMMEDIATELY converted into the final course when you are ready.

To briefly review, the critical thinking course consists of an overall animation to INTRODUCE the WHOLE COURSE, as well INDIVIDUAL INTRODUCTIONS for each separate story/scenario. These individual introductions are presented immediately before the scenario is viewed. There are three sets of questions, which immediately follow the discussion of the respective scenario/story.

The subject matter expert's template has a blank "introduction" page, where he/she writes how the overall introduction should appear, what words to include, as well as the pictures and phrases to feature. It also has 4 sets of THREE blank text pages, followed by THREE blank "choose-all-that-apply" pages. These places are where the subject matter expert places the story introduction, the actual story itself, and finally the story discussion/reflection. This is followed by the "error detection" question, the "predict-the-consequence" question, and finally the "correct-the-situation" question respectively. Unlike the information course template, this critical thinking template follows the EXACT SAME FORMAT as your final course. It is, therefore, not initially as confusing as the information course. This diagram illustrates the subject matter expert's template, into which their content is "poured". This diagram is ONE ITERATION, or 1 set, of the "4 complete sets" that make up a course . . .

Diagram of One Iteration

Overall Introduction

- In this space . . .
  place phrases, pictures,
  and words to include
  in the overall
  animated introduction

Place Story Heading Here

- Story introduction
  bullet point #1

- Story introduction
  bullet point #2

- Story introduction
  bullet point #3

Place Story Heading Here

- Type THE COMPLETE
  STORY here in this space

Place Story Heading Here

- Story SUMMARY
  bullet point #1

- Story SUMMARY
  bullet point #2

- Story SUMMARY
  bullet point #3

Place "ERROR DETECTION" Choose-All-That-Apply Question Here

☐ Answer Option

☐ Answer Option

☐ Answer Option

☐ Answer Option

☐ Answer Option

Place "PREDICT" Choose-All-That-Apply Question Here

☐ Answer Option

☐ Answer Option

☐ Answer Option

☐ Answer Option

☐ Answer Option

Place "CORRECT" Choose-All-That-Apply Question Here

☐ Answer Option

☐ Answer Option

☐ Answer Option

☐ Answer Option

☐ Answer Option

This process (featured on the previous page) may be repeated up to 4 times total, for a complete, maximum-sized critical thinking course. Any more than 4 times may overwhelm the healthcare/medical student, with too much information. Thus, if more critical thinking material needs to be taught to your healthcare audience . . . CREATE ANOTHER COURSE!

Remember, fill out the template together with the subject matter expert. This will speed up the production process dramatically, as well as increase accuracy and quality.

The following guidelines constitute the quarters in Step 3, Expert Template Completion, assuming the course is the maximum sized module:

- 25% . . . ONE ITERATION, OR CYCLE, of the template is completed (filled out). One iteration or cycle is represented in the diagram in this section, which illustrates 1 set out of the 4 total sets in a complete course

- 50% . . . 2 (TWO) ITERATIONS, OR CYCLES, of the templates are completed (filled out). One iteration or cycle is represented in the diagram in this section, which illustrates 1 set out of the 4 total sets in a complete course

- 75% . . . 3 (THREE) ITERATIONS, OR CYCLES, of the templates are completed (filled out). One iteration or cycle is represented in the diagram in this section, which illustrates 1 set out of the 4 total sets in a complete course

- 100% . . . ALL 4 (FOUR) ITERATIONS, OR CYCLES, of the templates are completed (filled out). One iteration or cycle is represented in the diagram in this section, which illustrates 1 set out of the 4 total sets in a complete course

Developing The Scenarios

This step may, perhaps, be the most time-consuming stage of the critical thinking course production process. However, it should not unduly prolong the overall development. The following options should be considered, for portraying the critical thinking stories/scenarios:

- simple written (text) version of the story

- picture slide show (with audio or text narration)

- audio dramatization (old-time radio show)

- motion picture movie

Each of these options will now be explained, with detailed instructions . . .

.

Simple Written (Text) Version of the Story

Text is usually the least expensive, and the fastest, method to portray scenarios. In many healthcare instances, it is also the only option. For example, it may be impossible to "stage" a movie of a rare heart condition or surgical complication. In such a case, it may only be possible to portray the complex details of this situation with a text-based story.

Being inexpensive and simple, however, does NOT mean that "text" is ineffective or inappropriate.

In fact, you may discover, with a large number of your medical/healthcare scenarios, that this is the BEST FORMAT to get the point across and to stimulate critical thinking aptitudes in your audience.

The subject matter expert is the best person to write the story. He/she knows how to make the story plausible (realistic, not contrived and sham) as well as factual. Once the story is written out, then, at this latter stage, it may be appropriate to provide technical editing and assistance to make it flow better. This is the proper sequence for quality assurance in the development of text scenarios, during the critical thinking course manufacturing process.

Picture Slide Show (With Audio or Text Narration)

A picture slide show is also a fairly quick, and inexpensive, method to develop your scenarios or stories. These are very similar to those the slide shows used in the 1970's and 1980's, where a picture was shown and described (either in person or by a cassette tape), and the frame was advanced to a new picture, when the audio tape signaled with a "beep".

Today's modern, web-based slide shows are based on a similar concept, but are much more amazing and will work with virtually any hand-held electronic device or display. These slide shows can be adapted for a hospital auditorium or allied health lecture hall in a paper-based format with pictures and text story captions, similar to a comic book. The slide show can be narrated with recorded audio, streamed live over the Internet, or narrated live by the medical school professor in the classroom.

It may be necessary to take pictures with staged actors, or models posing as characters in the story. Alternatively, royalty-free stock photographs can be purchased for this purpose, and can be used to fulfill various purposes (roles) in the scenario/story.

If text narration is used on a given frame, remember to keep the narration-text-per-picture very low, so as to not overload the healthcare learners with too much information. If audio is used to provide narration for the pictures on each "frame", then a much larger amount of "information-per-frame" can be absorbed and processed. Indeed, it is preferable to use audio instead of text.

Audio Dramatization (Old-Time Radio Show)

Many people enjoyed radio dramas (the theater of the mind), which were popular from the 1930's until about the mid 1960's. The artists (actors) who produced these radio dramas, were very talented. These men and women were able to create captivating scenes by well-scripted dialogue, as well as fascinating sound effects. Scenes of ships at sea, comedies, people at work, etc., were all portrayed solely by audio with no motion pictures to accompany them. While radio dramas are not common today, they are still a very powerful means to portray stories and scenarios. They are usually quite inexpensive, and are very fast and easy to construct, especially compared to a motion picture. Moreover, audio dramatizations, or radio shows, are a very effective means of inducing powerful emotions in your healthcare audience. Inducing strong, memorable emotions is especially important if you are training your medical or allied health students to deal with controversial or life-threatening situations.

To effectively produce a "radio show" style scenario, it is very useful to first listen to some old-time radio dramas. There are a number of web sites and media players that offer FREE re-runs of classic old-time radio shows. It is well worth your time to perform a web search and find some free or low-cost old-time radio shows and listen to them. There are also many books on tape that utilize dialogue and sound effects, as opposed to just reading the story. Simply reading a story is much different than producing a "radio show" or audio dramatization scenario. Reading a story and recording it, however, may be the only option that is feasible and cost effective with your particular healthcare project. If this is the case, be sure to still use sound effects and appropriate background music, if possible. Also, try to have a reader who is exciting, and uses expression/feeling, when narrating the particular passage of text.

The first step to producing a fantastic radio drama for instruction, is to write the scripts. The scripts are based on the original authentic story, which was composed by the subject matter expert. Writing these scripts is a relatively simple process, since the scenarios are not supposed to be too long, and are intended to "get to the point" quickly, without extraneous details. Although a thorough lesson on script writing is beyond the scope of this book, here are a few important points to remember:

- write lines that are relatively short (2-3 sentences)

- write in everyday language that is similar to common spoken dialogue, rather than complete sentences with difficult vocabulary (written language)

- Indicate where narration is necessary, to paint a picture of the scene, and also indicate where sound effects need to be inserted

Purchasing and using sound editing software is beyond the scope of this book, however, there are many relatively inexpensive, and even some free and open-source software programs, which can record and edit your radio dramatization. Be sure the sound effects you use/purchase are royalty free, so as to avoid any copyright infringements!

Motion Picture Movie

A motion picture is likely to be the most time-consuming alternative for portraying a story or scenario, but it may also be the most rewarding and effective. This is especially true if the healthcare procedure, skill, or situation is difficult to explain clearly with text and necessitates a video for effective learning to take place.

Depending on the budget of your hospital, medical school or allied health program, a motion picture may or may not be practical. However, since each scenario or short story should be short and to the point, the filming may not take very long. The most time consuming process may likely be in simply scheduling the actors, the time(s) to shoot, and the props.

Finding actors should not be a difficult process. The best actors for most, if not all, hospital training, are usually the actual allied health employees in the respective departments. For example, if your film is about correction action(s) performed by a radiology technician, then the best actors for the film are probably the actual radiology technicians themselves.

Scheduling times to shoot the films may be a balancing act between when certain areas of the hospital are available (e.g. MRI rooms, operating tables), and when the busy hospital employees, who are also highly paid, can fit filming into their important schedule. These obstacles should not, however, stop or slow the production of an effective motion picture. Although it is inconvenient at times, making movies can also be a very enjoyable, fun and humorous process for all persons involved. Moreover, motion pictures effectively help learners to hear, see and apply their skills in real-life healthcare situations. This medium cuts down immensely on the amount of text!

When producing a motion picture, be sure to follow the tips for script writing listed under the previous section on audio dramatizations. In addition to these tips, be sure to also include what the scene must look like, what each person should be wearing, in order to look "realistic", and where one scene ends and the other begins.

Script writing is not a complicated process, and can be done effectively by most people (even subject matter experts), with some practice. Although script writing is beyond the scope of this book, it would be worthwhile to purchase a good book as a reference for script writing and movie/theater production, especially if you choose to frequently use this medium to portray your healthcare scenarios.

Video editing software programs can be very easy and simple to use. Many of these are quite inexpensive. There are also some software programs that are very expensive, and are used for more of the "high-level" TV commercials and "big-time" movies. It is not necessary to purchase a super expensive video editing program such as this, in order to produce an amazing healthcare critical thinking movie. While this is certainly an option, it is not a necessity.

Cameras, camcorders and filming equipment for capturing and digitizing motion pictures can also be purchased very inexpensively. Conversely, these items can be found for a mega high price. An inexpensive camcorder can produce fantastic critical thinking movies for medical schools, nursing programs, allied health programs, and hospitals. It is completely acceptable to purchase expensive equipment, but this is not necessary in order to have high quality learning.

The following guidelines constitute the quarters in Step 4 (Develop Scenarios), in the critical thinking course production process:

- 25% . . . Stories are decided on, and there is a general idea of what they involve in terms of the media needed to portray them

- 50% . . . Stories are completely written out by the subject matter expert, and the medium of portrayal is decided upon

- 75% . . . All scripts for the stories are written (if applicable to the particular medium). Actors and other key persons are arranged and scheduled. Appropriate materials (sound effects, stock photos, video editing software, sound editing software, sound recording equipment, camera equipment) are all purchased, learned, and ready to use

- 100% . . . The scenarios are completely produced and edited and in final form

Conversion of Expert Template Into Final Course

With the scenario production complete, this step is likely to be the easiest! Just like in the information course, this step consists of a fair amount of "copying and pasting" of content from the subject matter expert's template, into your final course shell.

Your final course shell should already have the fantastic graphic design scheme, which is demanded by the professional healthcare environment you are serving.

Likewise, the navigation scheme and other interface elements must already be constructed, prior to "pouring" the content into your finished course shell. If the course is a live lecture for an allied health program, nursing school or medical lecture, then the paper-based final course should look professional, and have all the elements of powerful instruction already built into the paper interface. Thus, all that is required is to "pour" the subject matter expert's content into your empty final course housing. The order of elements in the subject matter expert's template is identical to that of your final course shell, so there is no need to re-order elements like in the information course.

Your final, professional-looking healthcare course shell can be built using an authoring program, if it is computer-based training, or in a presentation or word processing program, if it is for a live medical audience. There are free, open source programs for constructing both your computer-based and paper-based final course shells.

The following guidelines constitute the quarters in Step 5 (conversion of expert template into final course), assuming the course is the maximum size:

- 25% . . . 1 subject matter expert template has been "poured" into your final critical thinking course housing, and is ready to go for your healthcare audience

- 50% . . . 2 subject matter expert templates have been "poured" into your final critical thinking course housings, and are ready to go for your healthcare audience

- 75% . . . 3 subject matter expert templates have been "poured" into your final critical thinking course housings, and are ready to go for your healthcare audience

- 100% . . . 4 subject matter expert templates have been "poured" into your final critical thinking course housings, and are ready to go for your healthcare audience. At this point, your critical thinking course is completely done!!

This chapter outlined the production process for the critical thinking course. If the steps presented here are followed exactly, a critical thinking course can be completed in a very short amount of time, even within a few short days. Moreover, this course(s) can be produced without the need for any unnecessary, time-wasting, beta testing. This is because everything will have been completed simultaneously with the subject matter expert, and continuously evaluated during every step of the production process.

The critical thinking course, when combined with with the information course, helps to ensure that your healthcare students will memorize material, as well as problem solve with it at a deep level. These two courses constitute a complete program of powerful instruction, which will improve performance within the hospital workplace, and ultimately better the quality of care for the patient!

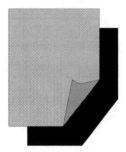

Chapter 7

Powerful Training For Complex Situations

At this point, you understand the purpose of an information course, as well as the aim of a critical thinking course. You know how to build multiple choice questions (learning interactions), which cultivate "information" or memorization skills. You are now well prepared to construct critical thinking learning interactions, which teach healthcare students to predict, problem solve and analyze. Having these instructional development skills as a prerequisite foundation, will ready you for a final (and amazing) task . . . an opportunity to use your newly acquired knowledge and skills, and apply them to the task of molding your hospital employees and medical students into SEASONED EXPERTS!

Instead of merely becoming "proficient" at memorizing a set of facts, or "satisfactory" at performing some skill, your healthcare learners will become wise, powerfully-trained experts. They will react with precision and accuracy in highly complex, dangerous and stressful situations.

It is important to remember, however, that your healthcare learners should NOT participate in any of the activities presented in this chapter, until they have participated in at least one "information" course and a minimum of one "critical thinking" course, within his/her respective medical/nursing/allied health sub-discipline. Thus, the learning interactions presented in this last chapter are intended as a capstone, or last step, in the learner's journey from novice to expert. This capstone only has meaning, and relevance, when there is a foundation of information AND critical thinking course(s), in the respective healthcare domain.

This cutting-edge methodology involves constructing 4 sections of learning interactions for your healthcare employees or medical/allied health students:

- Foundations, Connections and Basic Transfer interactions

- Completion layer of NEAR TRANSFER worked examples

- Completion layer of FAR TRANSFER worked examples

- Final Comprehensive Verification

Foundation, Connection and Basic Transfer Interactions

These questions consist of 11 distinct types, with 2-3 questions for each "type". Thus, for this category of "Foundation, Connection and Basic Transfer Interactions", there should be a minimum of 22 – 33 multiple choice learning interactions (questions) for the respective healthcare domain that the medical, nursing or allied health student reviews (tests), until he/she scores 100%. The 11 distinct question types are explained below . . .

1. Question Type 1 . . . Knowledge Based Questions

   → These are simple recall questions, to review basic and key concepts. Text, movies, or animations appear on a display panel as part of the question, if the training is computer based. Otherwise, text readings or pictures appear on a sheet of paper as part of the question. After attempting each respective question(s), immediate feedback provides the healthcare student with the correct answer.

2. Question Type 2 . . . Analogies

   → Healthcare learners go through a series of multiple-choice questions, which are simple analogies. These analogies help the student to relate important themes from the lesson(s), often abstract ideas, to concrete associations in the real observable world. The feedback on these analogy questions will provide the healthcare learner with the correct answer, and ALSO explain WHY the respective answer (analogy) is the BEST CHOICE to form a relationship with the given idea in the lesson.

3. Question Type 3 . . . How and Why

→ These learning interactions require the medical students to choose the best answer option(s) in the multiple choice question, which explains HOW the system works, or which explains how "A" CAUSES (influences) "B", or which answer option best describes WHY the model of the biomedical system works in a given manner, etc. The feedback for these respective questions explain WHY the correct cause/effect model is the best choice, and also explains the weakness of the other answer options.

4. Question Type 4 . . . Detect the Errors (Near Transfer)

→ "Near transfer" refers to those real-life situations that are "near" or close to the scenarios described in the recent healthcare training. If certain stories are described in the critical thinking courses, and specific situations are mentioned in the information courses, then a "near" transfer setting would be an environment that mirrors the recent learning in those respective healthcare course(s). For example, if a radiology technician is learning about fluoroscopy in an information course, and also in a critical thinking course, and shortly after goes out to work in the fluoroscopy area . . . then this is "near" transfer. Multiple choice questions that are "near transfer error-detection" interactions, will require the learner to view a scenario that mirrors the healthcare environment he/she just recently studied, and to detect the errors in a "choose-all-that-apply" format. The feedback for these questions will inform the learner immediately what the errors were, in each given scenario (question).

5. Question Type 5 . . . Predict The Consequences (Near Transfer)

➔ For these questions the learner will select the most likely consequence, in a choose-all-that-apply format. These questions will present a scenario that mirrors a situation "near" to those encountered in an earlier critical thinking course. The feedback provides the learner with the rationale for the consequence occurring, and WHY it's likelihood or chance (probability) of occurring is high.

6. Question Type 6 . . . Correct The Situation (Near Transfer)

➔ These multiple choice learning interactions require the healthcare student to view a situation that is very "near" to those others, which were encountered in their prior critical thinking and information courses. The learner chooses the best options, from a choose-all-that-apply list of choices that "should have" been done. The learner imagines that he/she could rewind time in this "near transfer" situation, and decides what might have been a better set of choices, if the circumstances could be reversed and tried again. The immediate feedback on these questions will provide the healthcare student with the set of correct actions that should have been performed, as well as a RATIONALE for this set of actions, in the near transfer scenario.

7. Question Type 7 . . Practical Application (Near Transfer)

➔ For these question types, the healthcare student is presented with practical (useful, relevant, common, everyday) problems. These are fairly simple problems. He/she selects the answer(s) that designates the correct step(s) to solve the problem. For example, the nursing student may be presented with a common problem, which is regularly encountered when administering an IV to an elderly patient, using a standard protocol (sequence of steps). The "practical application near transfer" question may list all the steps, except the last one, and require the nursing student to select the "next step" from a list of answer options. The immediate feedback from these questions tells the nurse what the correct step(s) is, and why.

8. Question Type 8 . . . Detect The Errors (Far Transfer)

→ A "far" transfer situation is one that is non-exemplary, uncommon, unique, and is a "far stretch" from the training material. It requires creativity, inventiveness and innovation from the hospital employee, medical student, nursing or allied health learner. For example, a radiology technician may learn about how to handle patients of normal weight and height, using a regular x-ray machine, available at most hospitals. But, what about handling a morbidly obese patient, who could be severely burned by a regular x-ray machine found at most hospitals? How is this type of patient to undergo therapy or diagnostic testing? A "far transfer" scenario would walk the healthcare student through this type of story. For a "detect-the-errors" type of question, the medical learner would be required to identify, or at least make an educated guess, at what was performed incorrectly in this "far transfer" story, which was "far" from the situations he/she learned about in his/her earlier healthcare training courses. Learners receive immediate feedback about what the errors were, and are prompted to re-try the questions so they become familiarized with these new and novel "far transfer" environments. This is especially important because, in the real-world, it may take many years before they encounter such a rare, unique situation. Therefore, this training may be their only opportunity to become "expert" at handling such difficult circumstances.

9. Question Type 9 . . . Predict the Consequences (Far Transfer)

➔ With this question(s), the healthcare student will predict the likely outcomes that result from choices in both ideal and "less effective" scenarios, which are "far" from the training content recently studied. Continuing with the previous "far transfer" example, the x-ray technician would predict the likely consequences that the morbidly obese patient would experience, as a result of undergoing radiation therapy with a normal machine, and being too close to certain parts of the mechanism. The multiple choice question(s) would require the medical student to select the most likely consequences from a "choose-all-that-apply" list. The feedback on these questions questions would provide the learner with the correct answer(s), as well as a RATIONALE for each consequence, and an explanation of it's probability of occurrence.

10. Question Type 10 . . . Correct The Situation (Far Transfer)

➔ For this question type, the allied health, nursing or medical student is presented with a "far transfer" or unique situation, and and then asked to select what should (or should not) have been done, if he/she was in the place of the main characters in the story. The multiple choice questions require the learner to select the ideal set of actions that should have been done, if he/she could rewind time, in this highly uncharacteristic and uncommon story. The feedback informs the healthcare student about what correct actions should have been done in this unique set of circumstances, and why they are important in this particular case.

11. Question Type 11 . . . Novel Application (Far Transfer)

→ This is the VERY LAST question type, in this initial section (category) of foundations, connections and basic transfer interactions. For these questions, the learner is presented with "far transfer" problems, which are novel (unique, different, odd, weird, intimidating), and require him/ her to apply their healthcare skills in new ways and curious settings, to solve real-life problems. Learners are presented with fairly simple "novel" quandaries, and he/she chooses the answer(s) that represent the correct step(s) to solve the problem. For example, the medical student may be presented with a unique and intimidating problem of administering a drug into the spine of a patient who is drunk, violent, and known to have AIDS. The learner would need to ADAPT a standard protocol (sequence of steps) to suit the needs of this particularly unique situation. This question may list all the "uniquely-adapted" steps, except the last one, and require the medical student to select the next step from a list of answer options. The immediate feedback from these questions tells the learner what the correct step(s) is, and why.

Completion Layer Of NEAR TRANSFER Worked Examples

This section (category) of questions consists of super-efficient learning! The healthcare learner becomes EXPERT in reacting with best practices, during complex situations that are both unique and common in his/her area of medical practice. The learning is "super-efficient" because it takes place with worked examples. A worked example is when a problem is "solved all the way through", so that the student can simply "observe" how the expert performs the sequence of steps. During this category of questions, the learner GRADUALLY moves through a series of worked examples, and eventually completes more and more of the steps in the worked example, until he/she can complete all of the steps in the worked example in an EFFICIENT and ACCURATE manner. This sections proceeds as follows:

1. Worked Example, Completion Layer 1 (Near Transfer)

   → 98% complete, 2% incomplete

   - Learners are presented with a very complex and advanced (near transfer) worked example of a medical/healthcare problem, derived from their recent training. 98% of the problem is already worked out, all the way to the final solution. Only the last 2% of the steps, before the final solution, need to be completed. The multiple choice question(s) require the healthcare student to select the final 2% of the action steps that need to be completed. The feedback informs the learner what the final 2% of these steps are, and why these steps are necessary.

2. Worked Example, Completion Layer 2 (Near Transfer)

→ 90% complete, 10% incomplete

- Question(s) are in the exact format as stated above, except that 90% of the problem is worked out, instead of 98%, and the learner is required to select the remaining 10% of the steps from the multiple-choice options. Feedback is the same as question(s) above.

3. Worked Example, Completion Layer 3 (Near Transfer)

→ 75% complete, 25% incomplete

- Same as above . . . very complex and advanced worked example. This time, however, only 75% of the problem is worked out. The remaining 25% of the action steps must be selected by the healthcare student, from the multiple-choice answer options. Feedback is given in the same manner as stated above.

4. Worked Example, Completion Layer 4 (Near Transfer)

→ 50% complete, 50% incomplete

- Same as above . . . very complex and advanced worked example. This time, however, only 50% of the problem is worked out. The remaining 50% of the action steps must be selected by the healthcare student, from the multiple-choice answer options. Feedback is given in the same manner as stated above.

5. Worked Example, Completion Layer 5 (Near Transfer)

→ 0% complete, 100% incomplete

- Same as above . . . very complex and advanced worked example. This time, however, 0% of the problem is worked out. NOTHING is done. At this point the learner is prepared to select EVERY STEP TO SOLVE THE COMPLEX PROBLEM. 100% of the action steps must be selected by the healthcare student, from the multiple-choice answer options. Feedback is provided at the end of the problem. The student compares his/her complete sequence of actions to that of an expert, and is able to see how close he/she came to mirroring an expert's performance, in this complex and difficult situation.

Completion Layer Of FAR TRANSFER Worked Examples

This final category again involves super-efficient learning, however, the medical, nursing or allied health student is guided through worked examples in "very unique" stories and scenarios. The purpose of these worked examples is to provide the healthcare provider with the ability to react in with expert performance in awkward and unparalleled circumstances. The advantage of an educational setting (computer-based or classroom), is that it is possible to simulate these singular examples. Whereas, in the real-world it may take 10-15 years to observe such rarities, in the classroom or on a computer, these can be generated in large amounts and practices regularly.

Again, the healthcare learner will become EXPERT in reacting the right way, during complex situations that are unique in his/her area of medical practice. The learning is "super-efficient" because it takes place with worked examples, in the same manner and format as described in the last section. Each worked example is "solved all the way through", so that the student can simply "observe" how the expert performs the sequence of steps. During this category of questions, the learner GRADUALLY moves through a series of worked examples, and eventually completes more and more of the steps in the worked example, until he/she can complete ALL (100%) of the steps ACCURATELY. This sections proceeds as follows:

6. Worked Example, Completion Layer 1 (**FAR** Transfer)

→ 98% complete, 2% incomplete

- Learners are presented with a very complex and advanced (FAR transfer) worked example of a medical/healthcare problem. 98% of the problem is already worked out, all the way to the final solution. Only the last 2% of the steps, before the final solution, need to be completed. The multiple choice question(s) require the healthcare student to select the final 2% of the action steps that need to be completed. The feedback informs the learner what the final 2% of these steps are, and why these steps are necessary.

7. Worked Example, Completion Layer 2 (**FAR** Transfer)

➔ 90% complete, 10% incomplete

- Question(s) are in the exact format as stated above, except that 90% of the FAR TRANSFER problem is worked out, instead of 98%, and the learner is required to select the remaining 10% of the steps from the multiple-choice options. Feedback is the same as in the question(s) above.

8. Worked Example, Completion Layer 3 (**FAR** Transfer)

➔ 75% complete, 25% incomplete

- Same as above . . . very complex and advanced FAR TRANSFER worked example. This time, however, only 75% of the problem is worked out. The remaining 25% of the action steps must be selected by the healthcare student, from the multiple-choice answer options. Feedback is given in the same manner as stated above.

9. Worked Example, Completion Layer 4 (**FAR** Transfer)

➔ 50% complete, 50% incomplete

- Same as above . . . very complex and advanced FAR TRANSFER worked example. This time, however, only 50% of the problem is worked out. The remaining 50% of the action steps must be selected by the healthcare student, from the multiple-choice answer options. Feedback is given in the same manner as stated above.

10. Worked Example, Completion Layer 5 (**FAR** Transfer)

→ 0% complete, 100% incomplete

- Same as above . . . very complex and advanced FAR TRANSFER worked example. This time, however, 0% of the problem is worked out. NOTHING is done. At this point the learner is prepared to select EVERY STEP TO SOLVE THE COMPLEX PROBLEM. 100% of the action steps must be selected by the healthcare student, from the multiple-choice answer options. Feedback is provided at the end of the problem. The student compares his/her complete sequence of actions to that of an expert, and is able to see how close he/she came to mirroring an expert's performance in this complex (FAR TRANSFER) situation.

Final Comprehensive Verification

This is the very last category. This last section ensures that your healthcare learners are prepared, and have mastered the knowledge, skills and aptitudes to perform as seasoned experts. This final verification is nothing more than a comprehensive review of ALL the previous 3 sections of questions mentioned above. However, all of the questions are included together and are randomized. Both the order of the questions, and the order of answer options, are randomized.

Learners are presented with ALL questions from EVERY section. During the comprehensive "test" or verification, each respective student is not given any feedback until the very end of the of test. It is likely that there will be between 140 – 160 questions total, if each section has a minimum of ONE question per subdivision, as described in each of the three sections above. Learners will go through the complete set of 140 – 160 questions until he/she scores 100%. After each iteration of testing, the learner will have a chance to see which question(s) were scored incorrectly and why, with individual question-by-question corrective feedback. After this feedback session, he/she will immediately be re-directed to re-take the 140 – 160 questions again, to try and score 100%.

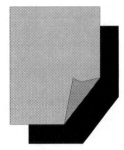

Chapter 8

Conclusion and Directions for the Future

This book has specifically defined elements of effective healthcare instruction. It has also clearly outlined a production process for building instruction and training in a short amount of time. Regardless of where you instruct, train, teach or educate, whether you are in a hospital, medical school, nursing or allied health program, your instruction can be produced quickly, easily, effectively, and inexpensively . . . by using the methods in this book.

By following the steps outlined in this book, you will better organize your lessons, reduce instructional preparation and production time, attain higher student evaluation scores, drastically reduce your stress load with regards to course management (keeping track of scores, grades and progress), and dramatically increase your student's ability to retain their knowledge and apply their skills!

The future of healthcare instruction holds great promise! We can rise much higher than the paltry public school systems we were raised in as children! We can learn from great practices of successful companies like Toyota, and from great minds of persons like Deming. We can implement these into our educational practices, to ensure that healthcare learners never feel like failures. We can make sure that healthcare learners realize their full academic and professional potential, regardless of the branch of patient care they choose to work in.

It is important to realize that nothing will ever replace a "live" classroom instructor, especially in hospital, medical school, nursing and allied health program. The live classroom instructor will always be an important component of a student's success. Technology, however, will greatly enhance the healthcare student's probability of retaining knowledge and will provide an amazing environment to practice their skills in simulated, virtual reality. 3D virtual cadaver dissections, cell phone/hand-held drill and practice exercises, animations, robotic surgery, tele-medicine, online learning, guided simulations, and many other technology-based learning tools will continue to emerge. These, and many other tools, will emerge at a dizzying pace. It is vital to keep up with these innovations, as best as possible. These will enhance healthcare learning, and should be capitalized upon whenever appropriate.

The future of hospital, medical, nursing, and allied health education is exciting and hopeful! I look forward to the future!

All the best in the journey forward,